The German Question and the Origins of the Cold War

Nicolas Lewkowicz

IPOC
www.ipocpress.com

IPOC di Pietro Condemi
8, Via Albricci
I - 20122 Milano
Ph.: +39-0236569954
Fax.: +39-0236569954
ipoc@ipocpress.com

Printed in the United States and the United Kingdom on acid-free paper

ISBN: 978-88-95145-27-3

Front cover: Marco Tamburro, www.mtartegallery.com

Contents

Abbreviations and Acronyms

ACC	Allied Control Council
AHC	Allied High Commission
APW	Armistice and Post-War Committee
ARP	Allied Reparations Commission
CFM	Council of Foreign Ministers
CBO	Combined Bombing Operations
CCG	Control Commission for Germany, British Element
CCS	Combined Chiefs of Staff
CDU	Christlich Demokratische Union
CFR	Council of Foreign Relations
COGA	Control Office for Germany and Austria
COMECON	Council for Mutual Economic Assistance
COMINFORM	Communist Information Bureau
COS	Chiefs of Staff
COSSAC	Chief of Staff to the Supreme Allied Commander
DMG	(British) Deputy Military Governor

EAC	European Advisory Commission
ECA	Economic Cooperation Administration
ECSC	European Coal and Steel Community
EM	European Movement
ERP	European Recovery Plan
FDGB	League of Free German Trade Unions
FEA	Foreign Economic Administration
FEC	Far Eastern Commission
FO	(British) Foreign Office
FOGS	Foreign Office German Section
GlavPURKKA	Main Political Administration of the Worker-Peasant Red Army
GNP	Gross National Product
IARA	Inter-Allied Reparations Agency
ICAO	International Civil Aviation Organisation
ILO	International Labour Organisation
IMF	International Monetary Fund
JIEA	(US) Joint Import/Export Agency
KPD	Communist Party of Germany
LIA	Level of industry (for Germany)
NAM	(US) National Association of Manufacturers
NAM	Non-aligned movement
NATO	North Atlantic Treaty Organisation

NGCC	North German Coal Control
NGISC	North German Iron and Steel Control
NGTC	North German Timber Control
NLP	Niedersachsiche Landespartei (Lower Saxon State Party)
NSDAP	National Socialist German Workers' Party
OECD	Organisation for Economic Cooperation and Development
OKH	Oberkommando des Heeres
OKM	Oberkommando der Kriegsmarine
OKW	Oberkommando der Wehrmacht
OMGUS	Office of Military Government of the United States
OSS	Office of Strategic Services
PPS	Policy Planning Staff
RB	Regierungbezirk
RLM	Reichsluftfahrtministerium
SED	United Socialist Party
SMA	Soviet Military Administration in Germany
SAG	Soviet Stock Companies
SDP	Socialist Democratic Party
SHAEF	Supreme Headquarters of the Allied Expeditionary Force
SWNCC	State War Navy Coordinating Committee
UN	United Nations
UNRRA	United Nations Relief and Rehabilitation Administration
WEU	Western European Union
ZEO	Zonal Executive Offices

I The Importance of the German Question in the Origins of the Cold War

The discussion and implementation of policy regarding the future of Germany from the declaration of 'unconditional surrender', made at the Casablanca Conference in January 1943, until the partition into two states in 1949, constituted the most important factor in the configuration of the post-war international order. Germany was given the most comprehensive treatment ever dispensed to a vanquished nation in the modern history of the international political system. The fundamental premise of this treatment was the acknowledgment of Germany's central position in the European political and economic order and its implications for the post-war international order. Germany had challenged the international order during the 1930s by rearming and gearing herself towards a war economy. Since 1938, Germany had redrawn its borders with her advance into Austria, Czechoslovakia, Poland and much of Western and Eastern Europe until the turn of the tide in favour of the Allies in 1942-1943. Germany was the only member of the Axis against whom all the major Allies campaigned together. This meant that at the end of the war, the United States, the Soviet Union, Britain and France would have troops stationed on German soil. The new balance of power system and the formation of the spheres of influence were created in Germany. Both the United States and the Soviet Union had significant vested interests in the political and economic reorganisation of Germany. The United States were fundamentally interested in fostering the political and economic conditions that would satisfy its 'grand design' for the post-war international order: the preservation and expansion of the free market system of exchange. Moscow's primary objectives were to prevent future German aggression and to extract reparations from Germany. These objectives were geared towards rebuilding its devastated economy and influencing the political process in post-war Germany.

The treatment of the German Question comprised Rationalist elements which stemmed from the Alliance that originated during the war, such as international law, diplomacy and the formation of spheres of influence. The treatment of the German Question was also informed by the pursuit of the national interest by each of the Allies. The implementation of long range structural interests spawned the conflict that would ultimately cause the polarisation of Germany and Europe into two camps. The treatment of the German Question also included the liberal elements which would overhaul the political, social and economic system of both Germanys and transform the society of states. The German Question would influence the post-war international order by making intervention and coexistence the primary institutions that would sustain the system of states. Developments regarding Germany would influence the order of things in Europe and the international political system as a whole for the duration of the Cold War.

Within the historical debate on the origins of the Cold War there are three mainstream traditions. The orthodox or traditionalist view, which prevailed during the first two decades of the Cold War, pins the blame on the origins of the conflict on the Soviet Union, adducing that Moscow imposed its hegemony on Eastern Europe and that the United States only reacted in 1947, in the form of Truman Doctrine and the Marshall Plan. The orthodox view sees security concerns and the protection of capitalism and democracy as the principal motivations of US foreign policy in the aftermath of World War Two.[1]

[1] See, inter alia, Schlesinger, A., 'Origins of the Cold War', *Foreign Affairs* 46; Feis, H., *From Trust to Terror: The Onset of the Cold War, 1945-50*; Ulam, A., *The Rivals: America and Russia since World War II* and *Expansion and Coexistence*; Kennan, G., *Realities of American Foreign Policy*; Mosely, P., *The Kremlin and World Politics*; Maddox, R., *The New Left and the Origins*

The revisionist school maintains that Washington conducted an aggressive foreign policy sustained by massive economic and military power, which motivated the Soviet Union to defend herself against the Western expansionism led by the United States. The revisionists see the need of the United States to invest abroad, to export the surplus of goods and to import certain products needed by the US economy as the prime objectives of post-war American foreign policy.[2]

In the latter years of the Cold War, there were attempts to forge a 'post-revisionist' synthesis. Rather than attribute the beginning of the Cold War to the actions of either superpower, post-revisionist historians have focused on reciprocal misperception, mutual reactivity and shared responsibility between the United States and the Soviet Union. According to this synthesis, 'Communist activity' was not the root of the difficulties of Europe, but rather a

of the Cold War; Ferrell, R., 'Truman Foreign Policy: A Traditionalist View', in Kirkendall, R., (ed)., *The Truman Period as a Research Field*; Taubman, W., *Stalin's American Policy*; Kuniholm, B., *The Origins of the Cold War in the Near East*; Thomas, H., *Armed Truce*; Kissinger, H., *Necessity for Choice*. While John Lewis Gaddis spent most of his career as a post-revisionist, he has recently switched to the traditionalist camp: see *We Now Know: Rethinking Cold War History*; see also MacDonald, D., 'Communist Bloc Expansion in the Early Cold War', *International Security*, Vol. 20: 152-88; Raack, R. C., *Stalin's Drive to the West, 1938-1945*. Traditionalists emphasising Stalin's pursuit of power and security over ideological ends are Woods R. and Jones, H., *The Dawning of the Cold War*; Mastny, V., *Russia's Road to the Cold War* and *The Cold War and Soviet Insecurity*; Halle, L., *The Cold War As History* and Spanier, J., *American Foreign Policy since the World War II.*

[2] See Kolko, G., *Politics of War*; Kolko, G. and Kolko, J., *The Limits of Power*; Williams, W. A., *The Tragedy of American Diplomacy*; LeFeber, W., *America, Russia, and the Cold War*; McCormick, T., *America's Half Century*; Fleming, D. F. *The Cold War and its Origins, 1917-1960*; Horowitz, D., (ed.), *Containment and Revolution* and *The Free World Colossus*; Gardner, L., *Architects of Illusion*; Bernstein, B., 'American Foreign Policy and the Origins of the Cold War', in Bernstein, B., (ed.) *Politics and Policies of the Truman Administation*; Alperovitz, G., *Atomic Diplomacy* and *The Decision to Use the Atomic Bomb*. For early critiques, see Tucker, R., *The Radical Left and American Foreign Policy*; Maier, C., 'Revisionism and the Interpretation of Cold War Origins', *Perspectives in American History*; Richardson, J. L., 'Cold War Revisionism', *World Politics* 24; Maddox, R. J., *The New Left and the Origins of the Cold War*. For recent consideration, see Leffler, M., 'Interpretative Wars over the Cold War, 1945-60', in Martel, G., (ed.), *American Foreign Relations Reconsidered, 1890-1993.*

consequence of the disruptive effects of World War Two on the economic, political and social structure of the Continent.[3]

This work analyses the German Question from a systemic standpoint. By examining the treatment of the German Question within the context of overlapping conflict, cooperation and legality, this work endorses a post-revisionist stance. The Allies pursued their objectives as dictated by their national interest. However, they also established in a highly complex framework of international law, diplomacy and a spheres of influence system. At the same time, they attempted to transform the post-war international order by creating a discontinuity with the Nazi regime and enhancing the scope of international organisation and cooperation.

[3] See Gaddis, J.L., *The United States and the Origins of the Cold War, 1941-1947;* Gaddis, J.L., *Strategies of Containment*; Gaddis, J.L., 'The Emerging Post-Revisionist Synthesis on the Origins of the Cold *War'*, *Diplomatic History*; Gaddis, J.L., *Long Peace*; Lundestad, G., 'Empire by Invitation? The United States and Europe, 1945-1952', *Journal of Peace Research* 23; Lundestad, G., *The American Non-Policy Towards Eastern Europe, 1943-1947*; Parrish, S., 'USSR and the Security Dilemma' (Ph.D diss., Columbia University, 1993); McMahon, R., *The Cold War on the Periphery*; Trachtenberg, M., *History and Strategy*; Yergin, D., *Shattered Peace*; Wolhforth, W., *The Elusive Balance: Power and Perceptions during the Cold War*; Wolhforth, W., 'New Evidence on Moscow's Cold War', *Diplomatic History* 21; Paterson, T., *Soviet-American Confrontation*; Pollard, R., *Economic Security and the Origins of the Cold War, 1945-1950*. For a recent discussion of post-revisionism, see 'The Origins of the Cold War: A Symposium', led off by Howard Jones and Randall Woods's 'Origins of the Cold War in Europe and the Near East: Recent Historiography and the National Security Imperative', with commentaries by Rosenberg, E., Stephanson, R. and Berstein, B., in *Diplomatic History* 17, no. 2 (Spring 1993): pp. 251-310.

III American Structural Interests in Western Europe and the Revival of Germany

The policies geared towards the accomplishment of long range structural interests on the part of the United States provided the post-war international order with one its main elements of conflict. American economic interests in Western Europe were inextricably linked to the revival of Germany. For the United States, the fate of Western Europe and its industrial resources were vital to its 'grand design' for the post-war international order: the continuation of the wartime economic expansion. This 'grand design' necessitated the opening of Europe to American goods, capital as well as an international economy based on a free trade system of exchange.

The Nazi New Order called for a German-led 'autarkic, national-economic' system in Europe,[4] permanently secured by military means.[5] The opening of the world economy would prevent the emergence of warring blocs and propel the continual expansion of the US economy. American involvement in World War Two had brought with it a phenomenal economic expansion. The New

[4] See Kemmler, H., *Autarkie in der organischen Wirtschaft*, Dresden, 1940 and Teichert, E., *Autarkie und Grossraumwirtschaft in Deutschland, 1930-1939*, Munich, 1940, quoted in Berghahn, V., *The Americanisation of West German Industry, 1945-1973,* p. 27-8.

[5] See Gauleiter Gustav Simon, regional chief of the Nazi regime in Luxembourg, September 28, 1940, speech 'The reshaping of Europe' on the Nazi conception of a united Europe. Source 'Neugestaltung Europa', in Luxemburger Wort. 30.09.1940, No 274, 93e année, p.1. Also, Funk, W., *Verein Berliner Kaufleute und Industrieller und Wirtschafts-Hochschule Berlin*, pp. 17-42.

Deal policies of the 1930s were not fully successful in absorbing the unemployed workforce. Unemployment in the United States in 1940 was at 14.6% from the figure of 3.2% in 1929. The American economy had not fully recovered since the beginning of the Depression. In 1940 the gross national product per capita stood at $916, only a slight increase from the figure of $857 in 1929.[6]

The war created a massive expansion of the American industrial base and an inextricable link between government and the private sector. In the first six months of 1942, the US government gave out more than $100 billion in military contracts, more than the entire national product of 1940. The Ford Motor Company alone was producing more war material than the entire Italian economy.[7] The war also solidified the role of government in the overall running of the economy. The United States was able to pay about 45% of the war costs through taxation. By 1946 the national debt had soared to 130% of the GNP ($269.4 billion).[8] The expansion of the American economy during the war was impressive. By 1945 the United States produced half of the world's manufactured goods and held $ 23 billion in gold reserves. As the leading revisionist Kolko argues

> as a capitalist nation unable to expand its own internal market by redistributing its national income to absorb the surplus, the United States would soon plunge into the depression that only World War Two brought to an end.[9]

This view had been endorsed by Secretary of State Cordell Hull, who observed that

> unhampered trade dovetailed with peace; high tariffs, trade barriers, and unfair economic competition with war.[10]

[6] Figures from the US Department of Commerce, Historical Statistics of the United States (Washington, DC) (US Government Printing Office) (1961) quoted in DiLorenzo T., *How Capitalism saved America: the Untold History of Our Country-From the Pilgrims to the Present,* p. 139.

[7] Gordon, J.S., *The Empire of Wealth-The Epic History of the American Economic Power,* p. 353-4

[8] *Ibidem*, p. 358.

[9] See Kolko, G. and Kollo, J., Op. Cit.

The American vision for the post-war international economy informed the financial aid scheme granted to Britain. Article VII of the Master Lend Lease Agreement between the United States and Britain of February 23, 1942 called for

> the elimination of all forms of discriminatory treatment in international commerce, and to the reduction of tariffs and other trade barriers.[11]

After the war, Dean Acheson, Assistant Secretary of State, commented that

> the only hope of maintaining world stability, social, political, and economic, was to adopt measures which will lead to an expansion of production, consumption and trade.

William Clayton, Assistant Secretary of State for Economic Affairs, argued that

> world peace will always be gravely jeopardised by the kind of international economic warfare which was so bitterly waged between the two world wars.[12]

This 'grand design' was informed by the experience of the economic depression in the 1930s and the American involvement in World War Two. The reorganisation of the world economy would be based on interventionist policies aimed at preventing a recurrence of the outstanding economic troubles of the interwar period and was in itself an extension of the New Deal. The model of government intervention in the economy at home would be exported to the international economy as a whole. The rationale behind the Bretton Woods agreements of July 1944 was to contain and transpose the threat of war into the realm of international commerce. This liberal order would involve the lowering of tariffs, free convertibility of currencies and free trade that relied on fixed monetary exchange rates. An International Monetary Fund was to guard

[10] Cordell, H., *The Memoirs of Cordell Hull*, Volume I, p. 81.
[11] Preliminary Agreement Between the United States and the United Kingdom, February 23, 1942- http://www.yale.edu/lawweb/avalon/decade/decade04.htm.
[12] Kolko, G., *Politics of War-Allied Diplomacy of the World Crisis of 1943-1945*, p. 485.

against a repetition of the exchange crisis in 1931-2 by providing funds to tie over temporary balance of payment difficulties. An International Bank of Settlements would be established to regulate international lending. An International Trade Organisation was to create a free trade environment.[13]

This vision of a free trade economic order was incompatible with Soviet ideology. Berghahn argues that the emergence of two blocs after the war has to be seen in the context of a simplification exercise. Instead of integrating the 'planned' economies of Central and Eastern Europe, America sought to adapt the industrial centres of Western Europe and the Far East to the American model.[14] This 'half world' compromise can also be interpreted as a willingness to coexist with the Soviet Union. The structural interests of the United States in the post-war international order were of an economic nature. The Communist economic system of the Soviet Union ensured that Moscow, unlike an autarkic European bloc and the British Empire, *would not be in direct competition with American interests*. Pursuing a liberal economic order in the vital strongholds of Germany and Western Europe would not put American interests irretrievably at odds with the Soviet Union. Superpower conflict would be restricted to specific boundaries whilst allowing Washington and Moscow to pursue their objectives within their respective spheres of influence.

The 'internationalist' camp in the United States wanted to bring Germany back into the community of nations through its integration into a free market economic system. In order to attain that, the German economy (whose industrial potential increased exponentially during the war) would have to retain a significant role in the rehabilitation of the European economy. The occupation of Germany would give the 'internationalists' an opportunity to strengthen links with German industrialists.[15] The 'grand design' had as its most pivotal element the reconstruction of Germany as the engine of a free market capitalist system in Western Europe.

[13] Penrose, E.F., *Economic Planning for the Peace*, p. 351.
[14] Berghahn, V. R., *The Americanisation of West German Industry, 1945-1973*, pp. 72-3.
[15] *Ibidem*, pp. 36-7.

This thinking stemmed back to wartime policy. In the early months of 1942, a set of intra-divisional committees of the State Department concluded that German industry and markets were essential to the revival of Europe and the establishment of a free enterprise economy. Curtailing German economic power would deprive the Continent of an economic system of exchange and create pressure for socialist state planning.[16] A report by William Diebold Jr., of the Council on Foreign Relations, suggested that nothing should be done

> to damage the efficiency of Germany's productive plants, which should play an important role in West European prosperity.[17]

Diebold had in mind the maintenance of the industrial network that could produce reparation goods for Europe. The State Department planners stressed the virtues of economic integration and the dependence of Germany upon the markets and resources of Western Europe.

The state of war had not deterred the business community in the United States from continuing their trade with Nazi Germany. By late 1941, the size of American investments in Nazi Germany amounted to $475 million. Main American firms like Standard Oil, Ford and ITT as well as the banking community, continued to do business with Nazi Germany during the war.[18] The contribution made by American capitalism before 1940 was crucial in the construction of the German war machine. For instance, in 1934 Germany produced domestically only 300,000 tons of natural petroleum products and less than 800,000 tons of synthetic gasoline. By 1944, after the transfer of Standard Oil of New Jersey hydrogenation patents and technology to I. G. Farben (used to produce synthetic gasoline from coal), Germany produced about 6 1/2 million tons of oil, of which 85% was synthetic oil. Furthermore, the control of synthetic oil output in Germany was held by the I. G. Farben

[16] Eisenberg, C. W., *Drawing the line: the American decision to divide Germany, 1944-1949*, p. 18.
[17] *Ibidem,* p. 20.
[18] See Higham, C, *Trading with the Enemy-An Exposé of the Nazi-American Money Plot, 1933-1949*. Also, Wallace, M., *American Axis: Henry Ford, Charles Lindbergh, and the rise of the Third Reich*.

subsidiary, Braunkohle-Benzin A. G. The I. G. Farben cartel itself was created in 1926 with Wall Street financial assistance.[19]

Economic considerations worked against the idea of dismembering Germany after the war. The most extreme pro-dismemberment view was presented by Harry Morgenthau, Jr, Secretary of the Treasury, to the President in September 1944. Roosevelt engineered the creation of a special Cabinet Committee on Germany composed of himself, Morgenthau, Hull and Stimson and Hopkins. The Cabinet Committee was given the task of looking into the German problem in order to make recommendations to Roosevelt on the issue prior to his departure for the Quebec Conference. The Morgenthau Plan called for the demilitarisation of Germany and the establishment of new boundaries, with Poland and the Soviet Union annexing parts of East Prussia and Silesia and France the Saar. The Plan placed the Ruhr under international jurisdiction. It also called for the partition of Germany into two states: a Northern German state, made up of old Prussia, Saxony, Thuringia and several smaller states and a Southern German state, including Bavaria, Württemberg, Baden and some smaller areas. The internationalisation of the Ruhr was to be accomplished by dismantling its industrial plants and its equipment transported to the United Nations (i.e, the wartime Allies) as restitution. The Morgenthau Plan also suggested adequate controls over the German economy for at least twenty years. These included land reform and reparations by the transfer of German territory and German private rights in industrial property, by forced German labour outside Germany and by confiscation of German assets outside Germany. The Plan also envisaged that the policing and civil administration of Germany could be carried out by Germany's neighbours (including the Soviet Union), and the withdrawal of American troops in a relatively short period of time.[20] Proponents of the plan stressed that the Morgenthau Plan would have removed the threat of Germany dominating Europe or attempting to conquer

[19] Kilgore to Howard K. Ambruster, February 29, 1944, Harley M. Kilgore Papers, West Virginia and Regional History Collection, West Virginia University, Morgantown.
[20] Morgenthau to Roosevelt, Suggested Post Surrender Program for Germany, September 5, 1944, FRUS, Conference at Quebec 1944, pp. 101-8.

the world, capture German markets for the British and provide industrial plants for the victims of Nazi aggression.[21]

The Morgenthau Plan entailed the economic rehabilitation of the Soviet Union through reparations and the extension of massive economic aid to the Moscow, possibly in the hope that Stalin would not need to block off and exploit Eastern Europe to reconstruct the Soviet economy. Morgenthau acknowledged in an unsent memorandum prepared on January 10, 1945, that those who opposed the Plan were moved 'by fear of Russia and Communism'. The idea of a bulwark against Bolshevism was one of the factors that brought the war. He also argued that the American position on the German problem could be a make or break factor in engendering trust or distrust between the Soviet Union and the United States.[22]

In late 1946 the Council of Foreign Relations (CFR) established a study group on Germany headed by Allan Dulles, which included John McCloy, John Galbraith, De Witt Poole and representatives from private companies who did business with Germany. Dulles emphasised the need to restore German industrial production. He also argued that 'satisfying Soviet security needs and [integrating] the West German industry into Western Europe' would be a source of conflict between the superpowers. The idea of rehabilitating Germany was also endorsed by the American Association of the International Chamber of Commerce. Its study group recommended that the Soviet Union should be included in an all-German unit if it gave up demanding reparations

[21] Dietrich, J., *The Morgenthau Plan: Soviet influence on American postwar policy*, p. 12. Dietrich argues that the genesis of the Morgenthau Plan reflected a sweep of sympathy towards the Soviet war effort of which US officials and American public opinion were not exempt. In the mind of US policy makers, and the State Department in particular, the rehabilitation of Germany would provide the basis for a European economic order conducive to a free market system of exchange that would benefit the US economy. This is one of the reasons why the State Department was weary about the idea of the Treasury Department for the agrarianisation of Germany. If German self-sufficiency was to be eliminated, it was to be done only so it should be dependent on world/American markets. See Kimball, W., *Swords or Ploughshares? The Morgenthau Plan for Defeat Nazi Germany, 1943-1946*, pp. 44-5.

[22] LaFeber, W. (Ed.), *The Origins of the Cold War, 1941-1947: A Historical Problems with Interpretations and Documents*, pp.111-2.

from current production and agree to a free market economic system and free elections. It also emphasised the need to incorporate the Western zones of occupation into the Western European economic system. The study group frowned upon the idea of excessive decartelisation and denazification.[23]

There was a close link between the American business community, General Lucius Clay's advisers, his successor John Mc Cloy and certain German industrialists.[24] During 1946-7 American businessmen traveled throughout the Western zones of occupation. Berghahn maintains that it was due to the mediation of private Americans that directors of German firms were able to remain in their posts or reinstated. These included representatives of the National Association of Manufacturers (NAM), which visited the American Zone in June 1946 and had been given a briefing by the OMGUS Economic Division on questions of reconstruction. James Martin, a member of the OMGUS Economic Division, surveyed the situation in Germany and published a report in 1947, calling for the reinstatement of board members of German companies. Martin also argued that German industry should be turned into a bulwark against Communism.[25]

Fearing another economic depression, the American business community deemed the reconstruction of Germany and a prosperous Western Europe as essential for the US economy. Leading businessmen like Alfred P. Sloan, chairman of the board of General Motors Corporation, indicated the need for an industrial Germany.[26] The link between American private economic interests and the German cartels was exposed in a report by the Army Industrial College. The Report emphasised the significance of cartel activity for the 'defense and security of the United States', underlining the fact that several American firms were tied to the cartels in fields most important for the war

[23] Eisenberg, C. W., *Drawing the line*, pp. 282-4.
[24] Clay was the military governor of the US occupation zone. See Bird, K., *The Chairman: John J. McCloy-The Making of the American Establishment*.
[25] Berghahn, V., *The Americanisation of West German Industry, 1945-1973*, pp. 82-4.
[26] LaFeber, W. (Ed.), *The Origins of the Cold War, 1941-1947*, p. 38.

effort.[27] Brigadier General William Draper, the head of the US Economic division at the ACC, was the vice president of Dillon, Read and Company, a company that had floated large amounts of German securities in the United States in the 1920s, including those from the Vereinigte Stahlwerke. A confidential report to the Special Senate Committee investigating the National Defense Program suggested that

> individuals with Wall Street connections and philosophy would not naturally be inclined to advocate forcibly and effectively a program of decartelisation.[28]

The US Congress earmarked the failure of the United States in enforcing the decartelisation of Germany. US Senator Harley M Kilgore, chair of the Subcommittee on War Mobilisation of the Military Affairs Committee and chairman of the Kilgore Committee, repeatedly warned during 1945 and 1946 that the German cartel apparatus, instead of being destroyed as required under the Quebec, Yalta and Potsdam agreements, was being deliberately protected. However, in spite of the dedicated efforts of Senator Kilgore, the connections between American, British and French capitalists and their German, Swedish, Swiss and other supposedly 'neutral' counterparts would ensure that the search for Nazi assets and Nazi business interests would in the long term be largely unproductive.

The Kilgore Committee heard detailed evidence from government officials, who revealed that when the Nazis came to power in 1933, they found that significant efforts had been made since 1918 in preparing the German industrial network for war.[29] The Committee devoted great attention to the impact of

[27] The Army Industrial College, Office of the Commandant, Washington DC, Report on Cartels, in Interdepartmental & Intradepartmental Committee (State Dept)-SWNCC-Decimal file 1944-49 Box 65 Entry 504.

[28] Confidential report to the Special Senate Committee investigating the National Defense Program on the preliminary investigation of military government in the occupied areas of Europe, November 22, 1946.

[29] Hearings before US Senate Subcommittee of the Committee on Military Affairs. *Elimination of German Resources for War.* Report pursuant to S. Res. 107 and 146, July 2, 1945, Part 7, (78th Congress and 79th Congress), (Washington: Government Printing Office, 1945), hereafter cited as

cartels in the development of the German military machine.[30] A special West Virginia edition of *Labor* magazine highlighted that

> Kilgore revealed that monopolies and cartels sabotaged Uncle Sam's preparations for war, and strengthened his enemies.[31]

The Ferguson Committee found that of the 500 enterprises that should have been investigated under the decartelisation law introduced in the US Zone in February 1947, only sixty-one were ever checked. From these sixty-one, decartelisation proceedings had started in only a handful of cases. At the Henschel enterprise, the greatest armament factory in Germany, proceedings were stopped on the direct orders of Clay in March 1948.[32]

The intricacies of the four-power occupation arrangement in Germany and the overall spectrum of inter-Allies relations had prevented the implementation of economic recovery in Germany. As late as January 1946 the State Department was in favour of a balance of 'punitive and constructive' policies in regards to the German level of industry.[33] However, by March 1946 the idea of a Western German entity was gaining ground as the four-power setting was not permitting the enforcement of US structural interests for the post-war international order. George Kennan (chargé d'affairs in Moscow and soon to become head of the Policy Planning Staff at the US State Department) was hinting at walling the Western zones against Soviet penetration and integrating them into a Western European bloc.[34] Kennan perceived that the Soviet policy on Germany was to create 'a People's Republic along the lines of Poland or

Elimination of German Resources. See Kolko, G., 'American Business and Germany, 1930-1941', *The Western Political Quarterly.*

[30] See Borkin, J., *The Crime and Punishment of I. G. Farben* and Maddox, Robert, *The Senatorial Career of Harley Martin Kilgore*, pp. 174-82.

[31] *Labor*, October 12, 1946.

[32] Burchett, W., *Cold War in Germany*, pp. 145-6.

[33] Acheson to Murphy, January 23, 1946-*FRUS, 1946,* Vol. V, *The British Commonwealth; Western and Central Europe*, p, 491.

[34] Kennan to Byrnes, March 6, 1946-FRUS, 1946, Vol. V, *The British Commonwealth; Western and Central Europe*, p. 519.

Yugoslavia'. He advocated an American policy 'independent from Potsdam' and pressed on the 'organisation of Western Germany'.[35]

The course of events in the occupation zones and the economic crisis of 1946 prompted the US policy-making machinery into action. Rostow refers to a meeting which probably took place on April 20, 1946, shortly before Byrnes left for Paris to participate in treaty negotiations. The meeting was attended by Secretary of State James Byrnes, Dean Acheson and Will Clayton. Rostow surmises that Acheson and Clayton argued that a division of Europe was being configured along the Elbe. They maintained that potentially divisive forces operated in the ACC. Subsequently, Acheson and Clayton devised a plan which had as its basic rationale a permanent American concern in regards to Europe and a general European settlement. They thought that Soviet, British and French officials considered the American foothold in Europe to be permanent. This would entail the formation of a Soviet bloc and possibly a Western European bloc once the Americans left.[36]

Economic considerations were pivotal in the formulation of US policy. The revisionist school emphasise the importance of economic factors in the formulation of American foreign policy during the Cold War. As Pollard argues, US policy makers had learned that American prosperity depended 'upon a thriving international economy'.[37] The prevalent view of the American establishment was that the United States, faced with a massive surplus of goods and capital, needed the reconstitution of Germany as a viable economic unit.[38]

According to Beschloss, President Truman, informed by the mistakes of World War One, perceived the need to reform Germany in order to avoid a drift towards Communism due to chaos and starvation.[39] The failure of the

[35] Kennan to Carmel Offie, May 10, 1946-*FRUS, 1946*, Vol. V, *The British Commonwealth; Western and Central Europe*, pp. 555-6.
[36] Rostow, W.W., *The Division of Europe After World War II: 1946*, pp. 3-5.
[37] Pollard, R., *Economic Security and the Origins of the Cold War, 1945-1950*, p. 37-41
[38] See Wala, M., *The Council on the Foreign Relations and American Foreign Policy in the Early Cold War*.
[39] Beschloss, M., *The Conquerors, Roosevelt, Truman, and the destruction of Hitler's Germany, 1941-1945*, p. 290.

Moscow CFM to keep Germany united gave George Marshall, Secretary of State after 1947, the impetus to launch the European Recovery Plan (ERP), also known as the Marshall Plan.[40] European reconstruction required products manufactured in the United States. In the immediate aftermath of World War Two, Europe did not have the dollars to buy these supplies. The United States had a sizeable trade surplus and its reserves were large and increasing.

Hogan maintains that the Marshall Plan was designed to promote Europe's financial, fiscal and political stability; to stimulate world trade and to forestall an economic depression through the expansion of markets for the US economy. The rationale behind the ERP was the creation of an integrated European market with the ultimate result of establishing a prosperous and stable European community, secure against the dangers of Communist subversion and able to join the United States in a multilateral system of world trade. It also envisaged a sustained political and military involvement of the United States in European affairs since even an all-European union would be too vulnerable to Soviet attack.[41] The economic revival of Germany was undertaken in accordance with the American 'grand design' for the post-war international order. Seen from this perspective, the policy to revive the Western zones of occupation through the implementation of Bizonia and the ERP constituted a demarcation line in the distribution of spheres of influence. Policy-makers in Washington acted according to a Rationalist pursuit of the American national interest. By pushing for the revival of Germany within specific boundaries, they minimised conflict and contributed to the formation of a workable balance of power for the post-war international order.

The decision to revive Germany was taken in order to rectify the reparations problem and the shortage of German coal being supplied to Western Europe as well as to minimise the costs of the Anglo-American occupation. The State Department knew that if Germany was to be revived, France and the neighbouring countries would demand compensation for the loss of reparations

[40] Trachtenberg, M., *A Constructed Peace: the making of the European settlement, 1945-1963*, p. 56.
[41] Hogan M., *The Marshall Plan- America, Britain, and the reconstruction of Western Europe, 1947-1952*, pp. 427-30.

and cheap coal.[42] In the Netherlands, the Bakker-Schut Plan called for large sums of money to be paid in terms of compensation and even the annexation of a part of Germany, which would have doubled the country's size. The Monnet Plan of 1946 proposed that France should be given control over the German coal areas of the Ruhr and Saar. The utilisation of these resources would bring France to 150% of prewar industrial production. The revival of Germany would therefore have to be undertaken within the context of an overall rehabilitation and integration of the Western European economies.

On May 8, 1947, Dean Acheson made a speech in Cleveland, Mississippi in which he stated that

> without outside aid, the process of recovery in many countries would take as long as to give rise to hopelessness and despair.

Acheson highlighted the fact that while before the war US exports circulated at a rate of $ 4 billion, they now totaled $ 16 billion, whith imports standing at $8 billion. Acheson concluded that the United States should

> push ahead with the reconstruction of those two great workshops of Europe and Asia-Germany and Japan

and that 'on the grounds of self interest and humanitarianism' the United States must take

> as large a volume of imports as possible from abroad in order that the financial gap between what the world needs and it can borrowed can be narrowed.[43]

As Acheson pointed out, the US State Department realised that a weak German economy was leading to 'economic misery' in Western Europe, which resulted in strengthening Communism parties and movements in those countries.

[42] *Ibidem*, pp.87-8.
[43] Speech by Under Secretary Dean Acheson at the Delta Council, Cleveland, Mississipi, May 18, 1947- www.trumanlibrary.org.

By punishing Germany economically, the United States was inadvertently helping in the rise of Communism in Europe.[44]

The most important studies which gave shape to the ERP were made by the State War Navy Coordinating Committee (SWNCC) and the Policy Planning Staff (PPS). The SWNCC and PPS studies, Clayton's memoranda and Marshall's speech offered a set of principles and an invitation for Europeans to participate in a joint program. The SWNCC report supported increased foreign aid for the ailing European economies and listed among the countries in need of particular help as Austria, France and Italy. It also argued in favour of German recovery and a coordinated coal program. The PPS reports were written by Kennan, who argued that an aid program would have to be large enough and last long enough to convince the Europeans that it would work. The report also concluded that the program should be organised by the Europeans themselves, acting collectively and including Germany and Austria. Eastern Europe should be invited to join. The long term aim would be to make Europe prosperous so that communism would have no attraction.[45]

On June 5, 1947 Marshall made his famous announcement at Harvard University, in which he stated that the preparation for war and the conflagration itself affected 'the entire fabric of the European economy'. He also stated that under the Nazis

> [L]ong-standing commercial ties, private institutions, banks, insurance companies, and shipping companies disappeared, through loss of capital, absorption through nationalisation, or by simple destruction.

He added that

> Europe's requirements for the next three or four years of foreign food and other essential products (principally from America) are so much greater than her present ability to pay that she must have substantial additional help or face economic, social, and political deterioration of a very grave character.

[44] Acheson, D., *Present at the Creation: My Years in the State Department*, pp. 241-4.
[45] Hogan M., *The Marshall Plan*, pp.81-2.

The undertone was for bloc-formation, as Marshall stated that

> it would be neither fitting nor efficacious for this Government to undertake to draw up unilaterally a program designed to place Europe on its feet economically.

Marshall also stated that

> any government that is willing to assist in the task of recovery will find full co-operation…on the part of the United States government.

However, he warned that any government maneouvring to block the recovery of other countries could not expect help from the United States.[46]

The Secretary of State's speech marked an important milestone along the road to a bipolar settlement. MacAllister argues that the early post-war international order should be viewed as a latent 'tripolar system.' He also maintains that

> the belief that Germany represented a potential third power whose defection or allegiance would determine the overall balance of power, as well as the closely related belief that a united Western Europe could eventually emerge as a third centre of power

exerted a dominant influence on American foreign policy after the failure to achieve a four-power solution at the Moscow CFM in 1947.[47] Clearly, the ERP enforced a bipolar outcome by marrying the 'grand design' thinking to the economic recovery of Western Europe.

The reconstruction plan was developed at a meeting of the participating European states in Paris in July 1947. The Marshall Plan offered the same aid to the Soviet Union and its allies, if they would make political reforms and

[46] Extracts from Marshall Speech at Harvard University June 5, 1947- http://www.oecd.org/document/10/0,2340,en_2649_201185_1876938_1_1_1_1,00.html.
[47] MacAllister, J., *No Exit*, p. 11.

accept certain outside controls. The plan was to be operational for four fiscal years beginning in July 1947. The Europeans sent a reconstruction plan to Washington asking for $22 billion in aid. Truman cut this to $17 billion in the bill he put to Congress. The plan met sharp opposition in the US Congress, mostly from the portion of the Republican Party (led by Senator Robert Taft) that advocated a more isolationist policy and was weary of massive government spending. The plan also had opponents on the left. Henry Wallace, former US vice-president, saw the plan as a subsidy for American exporters and sure to polarise the world between East and West. Opposition to the ERP waned with the overthrow of the democratic government of Czechoslovakia by the Communists in February 1948. Soon after, a bill granting an initial $5 billion was passed into law by the US Congress, with strong bipartisan support. The US Congress would eventually donate $12.4 billion in aid over the four years of the plan.[48]

The political aspects of the ERP were intimately linked to the rehabilitation mindset. In the 1980s, a new school was developed with some historians like Milward arguing that the Marshall Plan might not have played as decisive a role in Europe's recovery as was previously believed.[49] Such critics have

[48] Grogin R.,. *Natural Enemies-the United States and the Soviet Union in the Cold War, 1917-1991*, p. 118.

[49] According to Milward, it was the very strength of the recovery, sucking in huge volumes of American resources and causing severe balance of payment deficits, what created short term tensions. He also maintains that the ERP, although being responsible for the prevention of economic restrictions, did not make a substantial significance to the recovery except for maybe one or two years of economic growth. See Milward, A.S., *The Reconstruction of Western Europe, 1945-1951*, pp. 1-55, 91-113. This view is supported by Eichengreen and DeLong who argue that the Marshall Plan significantly sped Western European growth by altering the environment in which economic policy was made. The Marshall Plan era saw a rapid dismantling of controls in Western Europe and the restoration of price and exchange rate stability. This came about because to some degree the governments in power believed that the 'mixed economies' they were building should have a strong pro-market orientation. The Marshall Plan 'conditionality' pushed governments toward versions of the 'mixed economy' that had more market orientation and less directive planning in the mix. The Marshall Plan should thus be thought of as a large and highly successful structural adjustment program. See De Long B. and J. and Eichengreen B., 'The Marshall Plan: History's Most Successful Structural Adjustment

pointed out that economic growth in many European countries revived before the large scale arrival of US aid, and was fastest amongst some of the lesser recipients. While aid from the Marshall Plan eased immediate difficulties and contributed to the recovery of some key sectors, growth from the post-war nadir was largely an independent process. Arkes reveals that the actual financial impact of the Marshall Plan aid was quite small, at no time exceeding 5% of the recipient nations GNP.[50] The genuine investment value of the Marshall Plan assistance was not remarkable either. The largest portion of ERP money was used to cover imports of agricultural products, raw materials and semi-finished products. Used as credits for specific investment, mostly state projects,

> these funds supplemented domestic sources of capital, made it easier for governments to direct resources into politically desired uses and thus…strengthened state control over Western Europe's economies.[51]

Distributed in such a way, the Marshall Plan aid did not serve as an incentive for European governments to change their economic policies in order to attract private capital inflows, but instead encouraged them to continue with their internal policies of 'planification', demand expansion and premature redistribution.[52]

The ERP would create a permanent involvement by the United States in the political and economic affairs of Western Europe. Leffler highlights the political nature of the ERP by claiming that the Marshall Plan was essentially designed to stabilise the socio-political situation in Western Europe, to speed the incorporation of western Germany into the Western bloc, and to reduce

Program' in Dornbusch R., Nölling W., and Layard R. (ed), *Postwar Economic Reconstruction and Lessons for the East Today*.

[50] Arkes, H., quoted in Cowen, T., 'The Marshall Plan: Myths and Realities' in Bandow, D. (Ed.): *U.S. Aid to the Developing World: A Free Market Agenda*, p. 63.

[51] Food, fertilizers, and feed constituted 32,1% of all ERP shipments, raw materials and semi-finished products 48,3%; only 14,3% was used for machinery and vehicles. Cf. Kostrzewa, W., 'A Marshall Plan for Middle and Eastern Europe', *World Economy 13* (March 1990), p. 31.

[52] Kostrzewa, W., 'A Marshall Plan for Middle and Eastern Europe', *World Economy* 13, p. 33.

Soviet influence in Eastern Europe.[53] It was also designed to centre the European economic system around the revival of the western zones of occupation in Germany, a process which had started with the creation of Bizonia. The creation and implementation of the ERP had profound implications for the post-war international order. The ERP finalised the process of bloc-formation. The French managed to clinch a deal with Britain and America during the Moscow CFM on April 19, 1947 for an increased amount of coal to be exported to France, subject to revision by the end of 1947. The tripartite agreements signed in London on August 28, 1947 and in Berlin on December 1947-January 1948 ensured the integration of the coal production region of the Saar to France and the supply of coke for the rehabilitation of the French steel industry.[54] Furthermore, the Accord of the Six in December 1948 created the International Authority of the Ruhr, in charge of the distribution of coal, coke and steel.[55]

On June 28, 1948, on the eve of the currency reform in the Western zones, Bevin announced that

> the Six [Western European] Powers came to the conclusion that if this situation was to be remedied and conditions created in which Germany could profit from the ERP and reorganise her economy, it was necessary for a responsible German Government to be established as soon as possible.

In regards to the Ruhr, Bevin insisted on its potential to the 'contribution to European rehabilitation as a whole'.[56] On July 14, 1948 the United States of America and the US and British occupied areas in Germany signed an economic co-operations agreement, consistent with the Convention for European Economic

[53] See Leffler, M., *The Struggle for Germany and the Origins of the Cold War.*

[54] Poidevin, R., 'La France et le Charbon allemande au lendemain de la deuxième guerre mondiale', p. 371-2, *Relations Internationales*, pp. 365-77.

[55] *Ibidem*, pp. 373-4.

[56] From Bevin speech at the House of Common, June 30, 1948-From von Oppen, B. R. (ed), *Documents of Germany under Occupation 1945-1954*. Issued under the auspices of the Royal Institute of International Affairs (London, New York, Toronto: OUP) (1955), pp. 308-14.

Co-operation signed at Paris on April 16, 1948. The aims of the agreement were to achieve a 'joint recovery program…in Europe'. Under that principle, the military governors would ensure

> the promotion of industrial and agricultural production on a sound economic basis along healthy non-aggressive lines [and] the stabilisation of currency, the establishment and maintenance of a valid rate of exchange, and the balancing of government budgets.

Most importantly, for the purposes of bloc-formation, the agreement envisaged

> cooperation with other participating countries in facilitating and stimulating an increasing interchange of goods and services.[57]

The presence of the Red Army in Central and Eastern Europe entailed the threat of a Soviet advance into Western Europe. This threat compelled the United States to push for the integration of the Western zones of occupation with the neighbouring countries. This intervention implemented the principle of a liberal economic order in the Western half of Europe. The western zones of occupation were by the end of 1946 on their way to greater economic and political interdependence with Western Europe. A politically emasculated Germany facilitated the possibility of true cooperation within the framework of European integration. In this context, the revisionist interpretation should be seen in conjunction with the transformative effects brought about by the integrationist process in Western Europe.

American interests were implemented according to the demarcation lines imposed by the involvement of the Soviet Union in the war. Washington put into practice its containment policy in a 'defensive' rather than 'offensive' way. Cold War historians have argued that the 'containment policy' of the Truman administration was basically an offensive threat to the expansion of the

[57] Economic Co-Operation Agreement between the United States and the US and British Occupied Areas in Germany, July 14, 1948-*Documents on Germany under Occupation 1945-54*, pp. 318-22.

Soviet Union. It threatened to use force should Moscow attempt to expand its influence in areas that were not under Soviet control. Yet, it could also be considered defensive, because it let the Soviets know that the United States would protect its interests in Europe and Asia, but not make the first military move.[58] The notion of 'vital strongholds' was not detached from the criteria imposed by the spheres of influence thinking, pervasive in the superpower interaction over the German Question.

While the United States was prepared to let go of Eastern Europe, the need to incorporate Western Europe into its sphere of influence necessitated an interventionist approach. This selfish interventionism did not provoke an offensive response by Moscow. The Soviet Union refrained from actively supporting left-wing insurgency in Western Europe or properly endorsing the local Communist parties, ever so eager to respond to Moscow's diktat, as they did during the Ribbentrop-Molotov pact impasse. The unfolding of the treatment of the German Question contributed to the creation the 'West', as it was vital for the United States to protect its sphere of influence. The creation of a Western sphere of influence originated in the efforts to achieve a 'peace of sorts' in Germany. A permanent involvement in continental affairs would be the natural implication of the economic rationale behind Bizonia and the ERP.[59] In the long run, any desire to pull out of the Continent could not be compatible with maintaining a sphere of influence in Western Europe.[60]

[58] See Lucas, S., *Freedom's War: the US crusade against the Soviet Union, 1945-56* and Deibel, T., and Gaddis, J.L., *Containing the Soviet Union : a critique of U.S. policy*, Washington (D.C. and London : Pergamon-Brassey's International Defense) (1987).

[59] Nevertheless, Ireland points out that 'until the creation of the NATO structure and the assignment of US ground forces to that organisation, none of the American policies for Europe, as revolutionary as they were, implied permanent American involvement in continental affairs'. Ireland, T., *Creating the Entangling Alliance*, p. 183. The idea of a 'third independent centre of power' in order to correct the 'geopolitical disbalance' was also mentioned by Kennan. See Kennan, G., *Memoirs, 1925-50*, p. 463.

[60] Leffler and Lundestad have argued that America was intent on preventing the emergence of a 'third force' or an independent center of power on the continent. According to Leffler 'neither an integrated Europe nor a united Germany nor an independent Japan' could have been allowed to emerge as a third force or a neutral bloc. See Leffler, M., *A Preponderance of Power*, p. 17 and

Intervention in Western Germany and Europe adhered to the fundamental principles guiding US policy. As such, it became one of the two prongs in the demarcation line that created the spheres of influence. No other stronghold was more important than Germany in this demarcation process. The bipolar outcome in Germany created policy for the rest of Western Europe and conditioned the interaction with the Soviet bloc.

Lundestad, G., *"Empire" by Integration: The United States and European Integration, 1945-1997*, pp. 4, 54-57.

III Ideology and the Enforcement of American Structural Interests

Ideology was one of the main transformative elements of the post-war society of states. Ideological concerns had informed the Western response to the Bolshevik Revolution in 1917. Western European and American forces aided the White side during the Russian Civil War (1917-20) and occupied parts of Russia. The Western European powers had turned a blind eye to Mussolini, Franco and the assortment of dictatorships that sprawled across Europe during the 1920s and 1930s. They also built a *cordon sanitaire* against the Soviet Union through a series of military treaties.

The Soviet Union had a highly authoritarian political system under the leadership of a brutal dictator and an economic system that was diametrically opposed to that of the Western Allies. In the late 1920s, the Soviet Union embarked upon a process of war-orientated industrialisation. Stalin signed a non-aggression pact with Hitler in 1939, sharing the spoils of Poland with the Führer and, to an extent, facilitating the Reich's march into Western Europe in 1940. This general context of suspicion clouded the spectrum of inter-Allied relations and spilled over to the issues pertaining to Germany where the Allies had diverging interests. Adding an alternative dimension to the view espoused by the orthodox and revisionist camps, one could argue that both superpowers had structural interests in regards to Germany and the post-war international order. Conflict unfolded because of the enormous amount of power which the

United States and the Soviet Union accrued during the war. The American stance had from the very beginning an economic consideration. The ideology of the United States was in fact, the protection of its economic interests. Following from this principle, it is possible to conclude that ideology became a tool for the planning and execution of the split in Germany and Europe.

From the American perspective, its most important ideological tool in regards to the German Question and the post-war international order was the policy of 'containment'. The notion of containment stemmed from wartime policy and it was informed by the rationale behind Washington's involvement in World War Two: the expansion of American economic interests. Containment responded to the political situation that arose in Germany and Europe after the end of the war. In January 1946, the Joint War Plans Committee projected that instead of seeking buffer zones along its borders, the Soviet Union wanted to dominate 'the Eurasian landmass' and all of its approaches. In February 1946, the War Department advised Truman that the United States should provide help to nations threatened by Soviet expansion.[61] Furthermore, James V. Forrestal, the Secretary of the Navy, who commissioned a private study on Soviet policy in late 1945, concluded that the Soviets were committed to 'global, violent proletarian revolution' and posed a real threat to world peace.[62]

'Containment' thinking arose through the work carried out by the Policy Planning Staff of the US State Department, headed by George Kennan. The doctrine of 'containment' systematically outlined Soviet foreign policy intentions as directed

> to reduce strength and influence, collectively as well as individually, of capitalist powers' and 'toward deepening and exploiting...conflicts between capitalist powers.

[61] Gormly, J., *From Potsdam to the Cold War: Big Three diplomacy, 1945-1947*, p. 115.
[62] Forrestal, J., *The Forrestal Diaries* (ed.), pp. 127-32, 137-140.

It also stated that if conflict would ensue, the Soviet Union would make sure that war turned into 'revolutionary upheavals within the various capitalist countries'.[63] Kennan's strategy gyrated in its first stage around the principle of 'containment'. At its core, containment had as its basic tenets the restoration of the balance of power, left unstable by the demise of Germany and Japan, and the Soviet encroachment on Eastern Europe. Kennan's 'strongpoint defense' rationale entailed the strategic defense of five vital industrial and war-making capacity centres. Priority was to be given to the economic instruments of containment as opposed to military build-ups. The ERP is a perfect example of the implementation of this tactic. The strategy also entailed the configuration of independent and self-confident centres rather than spheres of influence subservient to Washington.

The second stage of Kennan's strategy involved the fragmentation of the international Communist movement. The recognition of Tito's Yugoslavia is an eloquent example of this theory being put into practice. In addition to this, NSC 48/2 was set up to encourage a rift between Mao's China and the Soviet Union. NSC 58/2 encouraged dissidence among Soviet satellite countries. A third stage of this strategy entailed the transformation in the Soviet thinking by the acceptance on the part of Moscow of diversity in the international political order.[64]

Containment was aimed at advancing US interests more than to arrest an elusive Soviet advance into the West. By the time containment was formulated as doctrine, the vital points pinpointed by Kennan were secured from Soviet influence. The nature of the Soviet system made it incumbent upon Washington to formulate a policy which would demarcate the sphere of influence in which to operate. At the same time, Kennan's third stage of containment mentioned the 'diversity of the international political order' as a transformative element in superpowers' relations. By the time containment

[63] Kennan, G., Telegram to the Secretary of State, February 22, 1946- http://www.gwu.edu/~nsarchiv/coldwar/documents/episode-1/kennan.htm.

[64] Gaddis Lewis, J., *Strategies of Containment-A Critical Appraisal of Postwar American National Security Policy*, pp.55-74.

thinking was operational, the Soviet Union had proved itself capable of respecting the boundaries imposed by the spheres of influence system.

The policy of containment became the official US stance on inter-Allied relations in March 12, 1947, when the Truman Doctrine laid out the need to aid all countries threatened by Communism. President Truman's message to the US Congress referred to the Greek government's inability to cope with the Communist insurgency and established that the United States would assist Greece as well as Turkey in their fight against Communism. Truman proclaimed that the world faced a choice between

> One way of life...based upon the will of the majority, and...distinguished by free institutions, representative government, free elections, guarantees of individual liberty, freedom of speech and religion, and freedom from political oppression [and a] second way of life...based upon the will of a minority forcibly imposed upon the majority. [The Soviet Union] relies upon terror and oppression, a controlled press and radio; fixed elections, and the suppression of personal freedoms.[65]

These developments culminated in the creation of the National Security Act 1947, which realigned and reorganised the US armed forces, foreign policy, and the intelligence community apparatus. The Act merged the Department of War and the Department of the Navy into the National Military Establishment (NME) headed by the Secretary of Defense and created a separate Department of the Air Force from the existing US Army Air Forces. It also established the National Security Council, a central place of coordination for national security policy in the executive branch, and the Central Intelligence Agency, the United States' first peacetime intelligence agency.

[65] President Truman Address before the Joint Session of the Senate and the House of Representatives - March 12, 1947
http://www.trumanlibrary.org/whistlestop/study_collections/doctrine/large/documents/index.php?documentdate=1947-03-12&documentid=31&studycollectionid=TDoctrine&pagenumber=1.

The outcome of the Truman Doctrine and the ERP was the establishment of a Western bloc capable of arresting any possible Soviet expansionist aspirations. Western cooperation amongst France, United States and United Kingdom and the Benelux countries was furthered by the conference held in London on February 23, 1948. Close cooperation was established in matters arising from the ERP in relation to the reconstitution of Western Germany. In March 1948 the Brussels Treaty Organisation was established between France, the United Kingdom and the Benelux countries to help each other in the event of an attack towards any of them. On June 11, 1948 the US Senate passed Resolution 239, which stated the idea of giving the Brussels Pact military support.

The ideological underpinning of the US national interests contributed to the breakdown of inter-Allied relations over Germany and the international order but did not extend to the creation of disruptive conflict. The protection of the vital strongholds in Germany, Europe and Asia entailed the creation of a military and intelligence establishment which ensured the enforcement of US economic interests. This would have an enormous significance for the post-war international order as intervention for the enforcement of US vital interests would be one of the most salient features of the Cold War. This kind of selfish interventionism was manifested in the toppling of Mossadegh in Iran (1953), Jacobo Arbenz in Guatemala (1954) and Salvador Allende in Chile (1973), all of them responsible for threatening US business interests in their respective countries. America's involvement in the German Question originated this line of thinking. At the same time, as we will see in the following chapters, the Soviet leadership was equally keen to enforce its own 'grand design' on Germany and the international order as a whole.

The ideological overtones of the United States revolved around considerations stemming from the pursuit of her national interest. However, these ideological considerations served to uphold the enforcement of structural interests within a clearly defined sphere of influence. The intervention of the Soviet Union in the treatment of the German Question served as a balancing element in the nascent international order and therefore restricted the scope of conflict through the Rationalist boundaries imposed by continual diplomatic and legal interaction.

IV Soviet Security Interests in Eastern Europe

The second prong in the creation of conflict in inter-Allied relations was the pursuit of Soviet security interests in Germany and Eastern Europe. The orthodox perspective underlines Soviet expansionism as one of the main factors causing the breakdown of inter-Allied relations after the war. However, the Soviet Union enforced their security interests only in the areas where the Red Army had a foothold. This indicates a Rationalist element in the structuralisation of conflict: Moscow did *not* attempt to discipline Tito's Yugoslavia with an outright invasion or to decisively intervene in the Greek Civil War. In this security 'grand design', securing a foothold in Germany was pivotal to holding on to Eastern Europe. Quadripartite agreement in Germany would have probably forced a retreat of the Red Army from Eastern Europe, as it occurred at the end of the Cold War.

The region's emergent pattern was the setting of coalitions of national unity and the establishment of 'people's democracies'. This pattern was guaranteed by the presence of the Red Army, which precluded Western scenarios of conservative restoration. On the other hand, Soviet security interests were narrow and indifferent to socialism per se.[66] The 'national roads to socialism'

[66] For more on the National Front strategy see Mark, E., 'Revolution By Degrees: Stalin's National-Front Strategy For Europe, 1941-1947', *The Cold War International History Project Working Paper* no. 31.

strategy already characterised Communist policy in Western Europe in 1945, and from the summer of 1946 until late 1947 it also applied in the East. The actual development of the 'national roads' strategy varied. Elections ranged from thoroughly corrupt in Poland to genuinely free in Czechoslovakia.[67]

In spite of the existence of tripartite Allied Commissions, the situation in Central and Eastern Europe developed in the direction of sovietisation. Hitchins argues that the Soviet Union moved to secure its position in Romania sooner than elsewhere in Eastern Europe because Romania was the gateway to the Balkans and the Straits.[68] By February 1945 Andrei Vishinskii, deputy Commissar for Foreign Affairs, had demanded the resignation of the right-wing Prime Minister Nicolae Rădescu. The National Assembly opened on December 1, 1946 with no members of the opposition in the Cabinet.[69] In June 1947, the government secured the passage of a law giving the Minister of National Economy the power to control domestic and foreign-owned industry. Currency reform was pursued and all foreign currency and most of the gold was declared government property. In October 1947 the Communist and Social Democratic Parties announced their merging in a 'United Workers' Party' and members of the Cabinet from other parties were dismissed and replaced by Communists.[70]

There was a similar pattern of Communist takeover in Bulgaria, where on October 27, 1946 a second election was held for a Constitutional Assembly. Both Britain and the United States decided that election conditions had not been satisfactory. Georgi Dimitrov, a Communist, became Prime Minister. His government consisted of nine Communists, five Agrarians, two Socialists and two Zveno Ministers.[71] The elimination of opposition leaders was completed by 1947. The Fatherland Front government consolidated its position throughout the country and passed a new constitution in December 1947, which protected private property but gave the state wide powers of public economic

[67] See Coutouvidis, J. and Reynolds, J., *Poland 1939-1947*. Also Polonsky A. and Drukier, B (eds.), *The beginnings of communist rule in Poland*, pp. 1-139.
[68] Hitchins, K., *Rumania, 1866-1947*, p. 515.
[69] Tappe E.D., 'Roumania' in Betts R.R. (Ed), *Central and South East Europe 1945-1948*, p. 11.
[70] Betts R.R. (Ed), *Central and South East Europe 1945-1948*, pp. 13-6.
[71] Auty, P, 'Bulgaria' in Betts R.R. (Ed), Op. Cit., p. 37.

organisation. Industry was nationalised in 1947. Private banks, foreign and domestic wholesale trade and large-scale real estate in the towns were nationalised in 1948.[72]

Poland remained the most important foothold in Eastern Europe for the Soviet Union. The advancing Red Army had not intervened during the Warsaw Uprising of 1944 because of the Soviet interest in having a friendly government in Poland. Stalin had broken relations with the London Poles and recognised the Communist orientated leaders based in Lublin as the legitimate rulers of post-war Poland in January 1945. Moscow pressed for the incorporation of Eastern Prussia and Silesia into Polish territory, which made Poland a *de facto* occupation power in Germany.[73] As such, it was paramount for the Soviet Union to ensure Warsaw's acquiescence to Moscow's diktat. By January 1946 Poland started to nationalise its economy. Meanwhile, on May 10, 1946 the United States had suspended deliveries against credit of $40 million and $50 million granted in April, on the grounds that the Polish Government was not keeping its election pledges, especially in regard to freedom of the press. A referendum was held on June 30 with an overwhelming victory in favour of the abolition of the Senate, the nationalisation of industry, land and economic reform and for the Western frontiers to become permanent. The Polish State took over the key sectors of industry and all enterprises, including former German and Danzig Free City firms which employed more than fifty workers a shift. Certain manufacturing enterprises, especially food industries, were turned into co-operatives.[74] By 1948 the Soviet Union was Poland's biggest trading partner and, in the words of President Bolesław Bierut, it was moving from a 'people's democracy to Socialism'. Finance and transport were nationalised. Co-operative industries accounted for 85% of industrial output and employed three-quarters of the industrial labour force.[75]

[72] Betts R.R. (Ed), Op. Cit., pp.46-9.
[73] The Western powers seemed willing to allow the sovietisation of Poland. See Mykołayczyk, S., *The Rape of Poland: pattern of Soviet aggression.*
[74] See Ireland, B., *Poland* in *Central and South East Europe 1945-1948.*
[75] Betts R.R. (Ed), Op. Cit., pp. 152-8.

The takeover pattern appeared to be slower in Hungary and Czecholosvakia. In January 1946 Hungary had been declared a Republic and a three-year plan was implemented in August 1947. Although Socialist and Small Holder Party members remained in government, they carried little weight. The New Chamber, elected in August 1947, had 271 Government members and 140 opposition leaders.[76] Bohri argues that any 'semblance of restraint' belied the fact that the Communists acted in the spirit of Stalin's exhortation.[77] According to Bohri, the evidence suggests that sovietisation had been intended from as early as 1945, and it proceeded more rapidly and effectively than previously imagined.[78]

In Czechoslovakia, on May 23, 1946, in free elections, the Communists obtained 35% of the vote, which denoted a genuine pro-Soviet sentiment after the Red Army liberated the country.[79] By February 1948 the Communists, in view of the prospect of a defeat in the upcoming elections, staged an outright takeover. The Communists campaigned for the parliamentary elections to be based on a single ticket list, composed of National Front party members and then ratified by the electorate in a plebiscite. The Communist Minister of the Interior purged the police of its few remaining non-Communist elements. The reluctance of the Minister to reverse the purges prompted a series of resignations by non-Communist Ministers who left Klement Gottwald in virtual charge of the government. Anti-Communist purges ensued at universities, the press, professional bodies, the military and the civil service.[80]

The spectrum of Soviet economic domination in Eastern Europe was the subject of a Foreign Office memorandum, which stated that

[76] *Ibidem*, pp. 114-9.

[77] Bohri, L., *Hungary in the Cold War, 1945-1956 : between the United States and the Soviet Union*, p. 5.

[78] Borhi, L., 'The Merchants of the Kremlin: The Economic Roots of Soviet Expansion in Hungary', Working Paper No. 28 Cold War International History Project Washington, DC, June 2000, p. 1.

[79] Halle L., *The Cold War as History*, pp. 73-4.

[80] Rothschild, J., *Return to Diversity-A Political History of East Central Europe*, pp. 94-5.

> Russia's policy...[is] ruthlessly despoiling the countries occupied by the Red Army. Simultaneously, they are using their puppets to gear the economics of these countries to the Soviet machine... [T]hey are making exclusive commercial treaties and securing a predominant share in the control of basic industries from Germany and the Adriatic right across to Manchuria.[81]

Davies argues that Moscow ruthlessly enforced all the main features of Stalinism where they did not exist. Soviet 'advisers' and specialists were incorporated into the local apparatus to ensure standardisation and obedience.[82] As to the question of whether the 'people's democracies' were formally integrated into the Soviet structures, Davies maintains that the main clues are to be found in the fact that the International Department of the Soviet Communist Party

> could control the affairs of the fraternal parties, who in turn controlled the republics for which they were responsible.[83]

Eley argues that post-war circumstances were favourable to a Communist takeover. The destructive force of Nazism and the mobility of massed populations created a vacuum that would be promptly filled by Communist forces.[84] Unlike the Eastern zone of occupation in Germany, which underwent a full-blown process of sovietisation since 1945; until 1947, the political future of Eastern Europe remained relatively open. In some cases, strategic security needs and weak local Communist Parties led to direct Soviet control, concentrating power quickly around the Communist Party, as in Poland, Romania and Bulgaria.

[81] Memorandum by Mr. Warner, Foreign Office, April 2, 1946- *Documents on British Policy Overseas*, (London: HMSO) (Series I, Vol I) (1991)-Eastern Europe, August 1945-April 1946 p. 346-7. Lukacs argues that perhaps even after 1945 a more forceful American foreign policy could have change the political takeover in Eastern Europe. He cites American protests in Bulgaria, which delayed a rigged election in 1945 and in preventing from unduly tampering with the Hungarian elections in 1945 as examples. See Lukacs, J., *The Great Powers and Eastern Europe*.

[82] Davies, N., *Europe: A History*, p. 1100.

[83] *Ibidem*, p. 1101.

[84] Eley, G., *Forging Democracy: The History of the Left in Europe, 1850-2000*, p. 305.

Elsewhere, like Hungary and Czechoslovakia, Communists took key ministries but proved more cautious on economic matters than their socialist rivals. Before the spring of 1947, the 'national front' strategy (parliamentary democracy, national autonomy, and gradual transition) was still a viable option. However, a relentless sequence of events in 1947 (the Truman Doctrine, the expulsion of the French and Italian Communist Parties from the national government and the Marshall Plan) irretrievably changed the political situation in Eastern Europe towards sovietisation.

The process of balance of power making entailed that the spheres of influence would be carved according to the criteria imposed by the 'grand design' thinking. Adhering to the 'grand design' meant securing a foothold *only* in the geopolitical spaces deemed vital to the enforcement of structural interests. Lundestad argues that domestic economic radicalism (land reform, socialisation of the economy, etc) played little part in American attitudes towards Central and Eastern Europe. What counted primarily was Soviet economic domination. Economic domination came in the form of exclusive trade agreements between the Eastern European countries and the Soviet Union. Joint Soviet-local companies discriminated against other investors. In addition to this, heavy reparations to the Soviet Union, direct confiscations in the form of war booty and a general political climate of conflict and suspicion, strongly discouraged US investments.[85]

One of the salient features of the process of sovietisation in Eastern Europe was the lack of effective support for the opposition parties on the part of the Western Allies. This lack of support coincides with the general structuralisation of conflict. Western support would have intensified conflict over parts of Europe which were not vital to the American 'grand design'. This denotes a selfish interventionist policy on the part of the United States. While direct intervention was needed in the industrial core of Western Europe in order to prevent a left-wing takeover, Eastern Europe did not merit the same interventionist policy. At the same time, the Soviet Union was not willing to

[85] Lundestad, G., *The American Non-Policy Towards Eastern Europe 1943-1947*, pp. 318-9.

aid Communist and left-wing elements that could have overtaken the political system in Italy and France. The Tito break probably reassured the Western Allies as to Soviet intentions in the post-war international order: although Moscow isolated Yugoslavia, it did not attempt to invade the country in order to enforce adherence to Moscow's diktat.

The Soviet Union was able to influence the political process in countries where the Red Army was stationed. However, Moscow did not show interest in supporting Communist and left-wing takeovers in Western Europe. Lack of support for these movements went back to the appeasing stance of the Soviet Union in regards to Hitler's takeover in 1933 and the relatively weak support for Republican Spain during the Spanish Civil War. This *modus operandi* would ensure the basis of coexistence in the post-war international order.

The sovietisation of the Eastern zone put the German lands east of the Elbe in direct contact with the Soviet experiment following the aftermath of the war. This helped the process of bloc-formation, established according to a convivialist criterion. Bloc-formation would prevent a revival of Germany as a disruptive power. Both Germanys would be emasculated by the presence of Western and Soviet forces in their territories.

The sovietisation of the Eastern zone went hand in hand with the 'wait and see' policy of the Soviet Union in regards to German unity. But this policy did *not* preclude the Soviet Union from entrenching their interests in its zone of occupation in Germany and in Eastern Europe. Securing a foothold in Germany was the minimum aim of Soviet policy in Germany. The process of sovietisation in Germany was a test tube for the establishment of Moscow-orientated regimes in Eastern Europe. The very notion of a political foothold in Eastern Europe depended on holding on to a piece of Germany.

Loth derives from Wilhelm Pieck's notes about his talks with Stalin and the heads of the Soviet military occupation in Germany, that the preservation of a united Germany was a declared aim of Soviet policy.[86] Stalin thought that a

[86] Loth, W., 'Stalin's Plan for Post-War Germany', in Gori, F., and Pons S. (Ed.), *The Soviet Union and Europe in the Cold War 1943-53*, p. 24.

united Germany would not be Communist or even Socialist, at least initially. At the same time, German Communist cadres were told in March-April 1945 that the main aim was not to 'realise Socialism in Germany but...a completion of the 1848 bourgeois-democratic revolution'. The appeal of the German Communist Party (KPD) of June 11, 1945 echoed Moscow's exhortation, as it called for the establishment of 'an anti-Fascist ...democratic parliamentary republic'.[87]

In June 1945, the KPD announced that

> a policy which should force Germany into the Soviet system would be false, for such policy does not tie in with the conditions of development in Germany today.

Their aim was 'to raise an anti-fascist democratic regime, a parliamentary democratic republic, with all rights and freedoms for the people'.[88] This gives the impression that ideological considerations gave way to the goal of safeguarding long range Soviet interests. A Red Army invasion of Western Germany would have probably been successful, as the battle-hardened Soviets were more motivated than the Anglo-American in exacting revenge on its former enemy. However, an outright invasion of the Western zones would not have been conducive to the accomplishment of the Soviet aims for the post-war international order and would have created an unnecessary overstretching of scarce resources.

The Soviet refusal to accept ERP aid was another milestone in the path towards bipolarity in Germany and Europe. Jan Masaryk, the Czechoslovak foreign minister, was summoned to Moscow and berated by Stalin for considering ERP aid. Stalin saw the Marshall Plan as a significant threat to Soviet control of Eastern Europe and believed that economic integration with the West would allow these countries to escape Soviet domination. The Czechoslovak and Polish delegations were prevented from attending the Paris

[87] *Ibidem*, p. 25.

[88] Davidson, B., *Germany: What Now?- Potsdam 1945-Partition 1949*, p. 27.

meeting. The other Eastern European states immediately rejected the offer. Finland also declined to attend in order to avoid antagonising the Soviets.[89]

Moscow was aware of the political conditions attached to the ERP. The Soviet delegation to the Paris talks was told by the Kremlin to

> object to terms of assistance, which could entail any limitation on countries' sovereignty, or violation of their economic independence.

Moscow was aware of the fact that American and British policy included the economy rehabilitation of Germany, a refusal to pay reparations from current production and most importantly, that the Marshall Plan would operate outside the UNRRA framework.[90]

An analysis of the Soviet stand on the Marshall Plan allows us to conclude that Moscow prioritised the establishment and consolidation of Soviet control over Eastern Europe. Stalin considered the Soviet zone of influence to be the most important legacy of World War Two and was not going to make any concessions to the Western Allies in this area. The Soviet government regarded control over that sphere of influence as most essential for geopolitical and ideological considerations. The Soviet leadership saw the United States of America as its main rival in the international arena and was determined to prevent the United States from expanding its influence in Europe. Narinsky argues that

> the unbending and unconstructive stand taken by the Soviet delegation in Paris was largely attributable to the desire to prevent the West from gaining a foothold in Eastern Europe, which Moscow regarded as its sphere of influence.[91]

[89] The Soviet Union's 'alternative' to the Marshall plan, which involved Soviet subsidies and trade with Eastern Europe, became known as the Molotov Plan, and later, the COMECON.
[90] Parrish S. D. and Narinsky M., *New Evidence on the Soviet Rejection of the Marshall Plan*, pp. 40-1
[91] *Ibidem*, p. 41.

The Soviet 'grand design' for the post-war international order could only be accomplished by holding on to a part of Germany. The Soviet Union was eager to prevent the revival of an independent, militaristic Germany. The occupation of the Eastern zone provided the Soviets with a test tube for the sovietisation of the countries occupied by the Red Army. The occupation of a part of Germany gave the Soviet Union superpower status, as it gave Moscow the chance to make decisions on the fate of the most industrial country in the continent of Europe.

Ⅴ The Role of Soviet Ideology in the Making of Structural Conflict

The main long range aim of the Soviet Union in the treatment of the German Question and the making of the post-war international order would be to secure a political foothold in Germany and the areas occupied by the Red Army. This thinking stemmed from the Soviet involvement in World War Two. Overy describes the Soviet war effort as 'an incomparable achievement, world-historical in a very real sense'.[92] Soviet deaths during the Great Patriotic War exceed 27 million (40% of all the people killed during World War Two). These included at least seven million civilians and 3.25 million soldiers who died in captivity. The Soviet military effort accounts for most of the 3.25 million German military fatalities during the war. A further three million German troops were captured by the Soviets. German losses in the Eastern Front accounted for 10 million killed, missing, wounded or captured and the loss of equipment to 48,000 tanks, 167,000 artillery pieces and nearly 77,000 aircraft.[93]

The 'percentages agreement' agreed by Stalin and Churchill in 1944 (with the tacit agreement of Roosevelt) corroborates the fact that the split in Europe would evolve according to the logical pursuit of the national interest and

[92] Overy, R, *Russia's War*, p. 327.
[93] Duffy, C., *Red Storm on the Reich-The Soviet March on Germany, 1945*, p. 3. See also, Merridale, C., *Ivan's War: the Red Army 1939-1945.*

within the framework of cohabitation,[94] instead of being subject to blind ideological considerations.

Soviet thinking on Germany and the international order evolved with national interests concerns in mind. As such, it unfolded in a cautious and highly rationalistic way. Ivan Maisky, Assistant People's Commissar for Foreign Affairs, in charge of the reparation program, submitted a memorandum on January 11, 1944, earmarking as the fundamental aim of the post-war period, the creation of

> a situation which will guarantee for a long period the security of the Soviet Union and the maintenance of peace, at least in Europe and Asia.

The concept of 'a long period' was explained as meaning

> a period long enough for (a) the Soviet Union to become sufficiently strong to fear no aggression in Europe and Asia, and so that no power or combination of powers in Europe and Asia could even think of such aggression, and for (b) Europe, or at least continental Europe, to become socialist, thereby excluding the possibility of wars occurring in this part of the world.

The second section set out the primary conditions for realising this fundamental aim. Maisky stressed the need for the Soviet Union 'to emerge from [the] war with favourable strategic frontiers'.[95]

In mid-December 1944 Maxim Litvinov, chairman of the Foreign Ministry's Commission for the preparation of peace treaties and on post-war order, advocated the creation of regional groupings within the framework of

[94] Mark has stated the fact that the US State Department accepted the view of 'open' and 'limited' influence of the Soviet Union in key areas of Eastern Europe. See Mark, E., 'Charles E. Bohlen and the Limits of Soviet Hegemony in Eastern Europe', *Diplomatic History*, pp. 201-213 and 'American Policy Toward Eastern Europe and the Origins of the Cold War, 1941-1946: An Alternative Explanation', *Journal of American History*, pp. 313-336.

[95] Filitov A., 'Problems of Post-War Construction of Soviet Foreign Policy Conceptions During world War Two' *i*n Gori, F., and Pons S. (Ed.), *The Soviet Union and Europe in the Cold War 1943-53,* p. 7.

the United Nations but under the aegis of the great powers with interests in the respective regions. Litvinov emphasised that he was not calling for the establishment of spheres of influence. However, he did mention that the setting of 'security zones' would only entail mutually beneficial military arrangements between the great and the small powers.[96]

Andrei Gromyko, Ambassador to Washington, led the Soviet team at the United Nations preparatory talks. He wrote a report personally addressed to Molotov on July 14, 1944 entitled 'On the question of Soviet-American relations'. He began his forecast with a bold basic presumption: in all likelihood, after the war the United States 'would be interested in economic and political cooperation with the Soviet Union,' and such cooperation would 'greatly determine the nature of post-war international relations.' In support of this scenario, Gromyko adduced that the United States had

> broken away from isolationism and will remain actively involved with the world at large.

He predicted that cooperation with the Soviet Union would survive in the longer run because of 'US essential interests in cooperation'. Presciently, he highlighted that the

> industrial-financial bourgeoisie of the United States...would be interested in the prevention of Germany's re-emergence as a serious economic competitor after the end of the war in Europe.

Gromyko concluded that conditions of peace in the international political system would allow America 'the maximum utilisation of the gains and advantages already achieved and those still to be achieved before the war is over'. He also predicted that

[96] Mastny, V., *Russia's Road to the Cold War*, pp. 231-2.

> the US would be sympathetic to and facilitating in establishing bourgeois-democratic political (as opposed to fascist-type) regimes in Western Europe, and first of all in Germany.

However, Gromyko underlined the 'possible difficulties' in Soviet-American relations, including possible disagreements over post-war treatment of Germany: the United States was likely to be considerably softer on Germany (especially on reparations) than the Soviet Union. Gromyko also pointed out the 'the general ideological hostility of the American ruling class toward the Soviet Union'. He also highlighted Eastern Europe (including the Baltic states) as a potential flash point because of the concern amongst

> American government and business circles regarding the prospects of social change and of establishing Soviet-type regimes in some of those countries.

Gromyko also pointed out that

> the US aspiration to increase its influence in the Near and Middle East (particularly in Iran)... would not be in the interest of the Soviet Union.

Yet, despite this fairly impressive inventory of potential problems Gromyko remained quite optimistic about the future, stating that

> the necessary conditions are clearly present for a continuation of cooperation between our two countries in the post-war period. To a great degree these future relations would be determined by the very nature of the relationship which has already been shaped and is still being shaped during the war.[97]

The key issue then became the nature of such post-war cooperation with the United States. There were no serious disagreements amongst Litvinov, Maisky and Gromyko: they all viewed the post-war international order largely in terms

[97] Perlmutter, A., *FDR and Stalin: A Not So Grand Alliance,* 1943-1945, pp. 259-278.

of *a great power concert based upon some kind of a division of the world into spheres of influence.*[98]

By April-May 1945 Soviet strategy had two aims:

1. to consolidate Soviet influence throughout Eastern Europe and to exclude British and American interference and
2. to take 'territory which if necessary could be used for bargaining with the West'.[99]

Stalin was not only pushing westward but also trying to hamper the Allied advance eastward. He informed Harriman on April 15, 1945 that a major Soviet offensive was about to begin, but stated that its target was Dresden rather than Berlin. A week later, after the Red Army had already encircled the German capital, Antonov sent a message to Eisenhower in which he claimed additional territory as supposedly belonging to the Soviet area of operations. He stated the Red Army's intention to occupy the entire eastern bank of Elbe, along with the Vltava valley in Bohemia.[100] Pechatnov asks the question of whether this line of thinking, espousing clearly-defined spheres of interests, examined in conjunction with the 'half-world' thinking prevailing in Washington and London could have given rise to

> a better post-war accommodation between the Soviet and Anglo-American 'orbits', instead of the rigid balance of power which emerged in the early Cold War years.[101]

This possibility gives rise to a reconsideration of the orthodox/revisionist debate. The interaction which arose regarding the treatment of the German

[98] Pechatnov, V., *The Big Three after World War Two: New Documents about post-war Soviet relations with the United States and Great Britain*, p. 21.
[99] Kennedy-Pipe, C., *Stalin's cold war*, p. 66.
[100] Mastny, V., *Russia's Road to the Cold War-Diplomacy, Warfare, and the Politics of Communism, 1941-5*, p. 269.
[101] Pechatnov, V., *The Big Three after World War Two*, p. 24.

Question and long range superpowers' objectives at large, could have been geared toward the formation of a less conflictual international order. However, an examination of the political implications of American and Soviet structural interests seem to confirm the view that conflict itself was an important factor in the creation of policy. The war mentality that industrialised the Soviet Union and expanded the American economy during the 1930s and 1940s respectively, was partially responsible for setting in motion the spheres of influence which informed the international order in the aftermath of World War Two.

Stalin's election speech of February 9, 1946 amounted to a condemnation of the capitalist system. The Soviet leader argued that

> the war broke out as the inevitable result of the development of world economic and political forces on the basis of present-day monopolistic capitalism...the development of world capitalism in our times does not proceed smoothly and evenly, but through crises and catastrophic wars. Perhaps catastrophic wars could be avoided if it were possible periodically to redistribute raw materials and markets among the respective countries in conformity with their economic weight by means of concerted and peaceful decisions. But this is impossible under the present capitalist conditions of world economic development. [102]

Nikolai Novikov, Soviet Ambassador to the United States, hinted at the possibility of a split in the Alliance with the formation of an 'Anglo-Saxon' bloc hostile to the Soviet Union

> The 'hard-line' policy with regard to the Soviet Union announced by Byrnes...is at present the main obstacle on the road to cooperation of the Great Powers. It consists mainly of the fact that in the postwar period the United States no longer follows a policy of strengthening cooperation among the Big Three (or four) but rather has strived to undermine the unity of these countries. The objective has been to impose the will of other countries on the Soviet Union. This is precisely the tenor of the policy of certain countries, which is being carried out with the blessing of the United States, to undermine or

[102] Speech delivered by Joseph Stalin at a meeting of the Stalin electoral district, Moscow, February 9, 1946, from the Pamphlet Collection, J. Stalin, *Speeches Delivered at Meetings of Voters of the Stalin Electoral District.*

> completely abolish the principle of the veto in the Security Council of the United Nations. This would give the United States opportunities to form among the Great Powers narrow groupings and blocs directed primarily against the Soviet Union, and thus to split the United Nations. Rejection of the veto by the Great Powers would transform the United Nations into an Anglo-Saxon domain in which the United States would play the leading role.[103]

The sovietisation of the Eastern zone and the breakdown of four power control in Germany would contribute to the formation of a Soviet-led bloc in Eastern Europe. In September 1947, the Soviets established COMINFORM (Communist Information Bureau), an information agency composed by the Communist parties of Bulgaria, Czechoslovakia, France, Hungary, Italy, Poland, Romania, the Soviet Union, and Yugoslavia (but not the German SED). COMINFORM re-established information exchanges among the European Communist parties that had lapsed since the dissolution of COMINTERN in 1943.

Stalin called the conference in response to divergences amongst the Eastern European governments on whether or not to attend the Paris Conference on Marshall Aid in July 1947.

The intended purpose of COMINFORM was to coordinate actions between Communist parties under Soviet direction. In practical terms, the COMINFORM acted as a tool of Soviet foreign policy.

The Soviet response to the Truman Doctrine was initially cautious and some policy analysts suggested a possible participation of the Soviet Union in the ERP. After all, the Soviet Union accepted lend-lease aid from the United States during the war. However, Moscow quickly realised that an 'open-door' policy in Eastern Europe would find them in no position to compete with the United States. Therefore, on July 2, 1947 Molotov announced that the Soviet Union would not participate in further discussions over the ERP and advised the Eastern European countries to do likewise. Zhdanov had by then advanced his 'two camps' theory and the Central Committee of the Soviet Communist Party

[103] Nikolai Novikov, Soviet Ambassador in Washington, Telegram, September 1946- www.mtholoyoke.edu/acad/intrel/novikov.htm.

spelled out the criteria for building Soviet-style Socialism in Eastern Europe: a significant degree of Communist political and administrative control, nationalisation of industrial, transport and financial systems, land reform and a pro-Soviet foreign policy.

COMINFORM's contrast with COMINTERN starkly defined the nature of the post-war international Communist movement. The meeting was small, with two delegates each from Poland, Romania, Bulgaria, Hungary, Czechoslovakia, Yugoslavia, Italy, and France. The Soviet spokesmen, Andrei Zhdanov and Georgii Malenkov, were in charge of proceedings. Key notables (Tito, Togliatti, Thorez, Dimitrov, Gottwald, Rákosi and all general secretaries of their parties) were missing. The East Germans and Albanians were also absent. Neither the Greek, Spanish nor the Finnish Communist Party were invited, which denotes that Moscow did not want to pursue a revolutionary path outside their immediate sphere of influence.[104] The purpose of COMINFORM was to instil loyalty to Soviet foreign policy among the member states of the newly-established Soviet bloc.

The 'Tito split' began Stalinisation's final phase, from the summer of 1948 to Stalin's death in 1953. Stalin was furious at the revolutionary independence of the Yugoslav Communist Party (KPJ). After 1945, whilst Stalin was abiding by his wartime agreement with Churchill of non-interference outside the 'percentages' areas, the KPJ championed dictatorship of the proletariat against parliamentary roads, affirming international revolution and backing the Greek

[104] See Thompson E. P., *Beyond the Cold War*. Moscow's bloc building tactics did however expand into Asia. In return for Soviet material and technical support during the Chinese Civil War, and in deference to the established Soviet leadership of international communism, by late 1947 Mao had completely accepted Soviet bloc leadership in the Cold War. Soviet strategic probes in Asia commenced following the COMINFORM's call in late 1947 for revolutionary uprisings. At the famous Calcutta Conference of communist and revolutionary parties of the East in early 1948, the Soviets gave a green light to communist parties in Asia who were inclined to revolt. In the ensuing months of 1948, communist insurgencies and revolts of varying intensity flared in Malaya, Burma, Thailand, the federated states of Indochina, Indonesia, and the Philippines. The Indian Communist Party also attempted to take over a province in this period. See Macdonald, D. J., 'Communist Bloc Expansion in the Early Cold War-Challenging Realism, Refuting Revisionism', *International Security*, p. 169.

Communists. Tensions crackled at a consultation meeting of the Soviet, Yugoslav, and Bulgarian parties in Moscow in February 1948, when Stalin accused Tito of creating an alternative Communist centre. Stalin recalled Soviet advisers in March, denouncing Yugoslav deviations. When the KPJ defended itself, Stalin expelled Tito's party from COMINFORM.[105] The break with Yugoslavia demonstrated that the Soviet Union could not gain lasting control over any country in which the revolutionary forces came to power as a result of their own strength. Moreover, the highest priority in Soviet thinking about revolutions abroad was not the survival and stabilisation of revolutionary power but rather Soviet control over the new government.[106]

After COMINFORM, the Soviet bloc's international line had shifted to promoting a disruption of the delivery of the Marshall Plan aid by transportation unions and open confrontation with local governments. The French and Italian Communists returned home to lead demonstrations and strikes that led to a sharp decline in their popularity.[107] The rebuttal of Titoism also marked a shift in Moscow's direction of bloc policy. Tito was charged by the Soviets with the crime of nationalism because he would not allow Stalinist agents to roam freely in Yugoslavia. All ruling and non-ruling Communist parties, including the Chinese Communist Party, stepped into line by condemning what should have been seen as relatively minor challenges to Soviet leadership on the part of Yugoslavia.[108]

Moscow viewed interventionism as a mechanism to enforce specific bottom line security interests. According to Zubok and Pleshakov, Stalin

> wanted to avoid confrontation with the West. He was even ready to see cooperation with the Western powers as a preferable way of building his influence and solving contentious international issues.[109]

[105] Pechatnov V. and Earl Edmonson C., *Debating the Origins of the Cold War: American and Russian Perspectives*, pp. 126-33.
[106] Bialer, S., *The Soviet Paradox: external expansion, internal decline*, p. 185.
[107] Macdonald, D. J., *Communist Bloc Expansion in the Early Cold War*, p. 164.
[108] *Ibidem*, p.165.
[109] Zubok, V. and Pleshakov, C., *Inside the Kremlin's Cold War*, pp. 276-7.

Leffler argues that Soviet policies were merely 'reactive' to US policy, particularly the Truman Doctrine and the Marshall Plan.[110] The Soviet Union operated cautiously and with strict regard to the norms of behaviour forged through the diplomatic interaction with the Western Allies. The evolution of Soviet ideology unfolded according to the circumstances imposed by superpower interaction in Germany and beyond. The Soviet Union adhered to its own 'grand design', aimed at preventing encirclement by the West. The notion of vital areas of interest and the 'two camps' theory endorsed by Zhdanov, entailed an underlying idea of coexistence in the post-war international order. The ideological machinery which informed the Cold War was geared towards sustaining the structural interests of the superpowers. In this context, the Cold War should not be seen exclusively as the unfolding of conflictual interaction between the superpowers but also as the informing element in the establishment of norms of behaviour for the post-war international order.

[110] Leffler, M., *A Preponderance of Power: National Security, the Truman Administration and the Cold War*, p. 512.

VII The Establishment of Bizonia and the Sovietisation of the Eastern Zone

No other factor in the course of inter-Allied relations contributed more to the establishment of two spheres of influence in Europe along ideological lines than the treatment of the German Question. The originating factor of an ideologically-split post-war international society was the polarisation of Germany via the gradual sovietisation of the Eastern zone in the 1945-6 period and the setting of the Anglo-American zone of occupation (Bizonia). This process was decisive in generating the subsequent diplomatic breakdown at the Moscow Council of Foreign Ministers (CFM) in 1947. When the Allies met at the Moscow CFM to discuss the peace treaty with Germany, they failed to reach an agreement on the economic unity of the vanquished nation. Indeed, the vital questions of economic unity and the extracting of reparations, crucial elements in the accomplishment of a four-power solution, had already been decided through the occupation process.

The ideological divide created in Germany had profound implications for the configuration of the post-war international order. The main rationale behind Soviet post-war policy was to prevent the emergence of a resurgent Germany and encirclement by the West. The Soviet military authorities and Moscow-trained cadres began to sovietise the Eastern zone right after the beginning of the occupation through the nationalisation of industry, land reform and the merging of the Socialist and Communist parties. The Soviets kept taking reparations in capital from the Western zones, at a time when the German economy operated under restrictions in its level of industry. This situation effectively meant that while the economy of the Soviet zone of occupation was recovering, the Western zones were descending into economic chaos, creating the possibility of a Communist takeover west of the Elbe.

Political life was reconstituted in the Eastern zone before anywhere else in occupied Germany. The KPD (the German Communist Party) and the FDGB (the Free German Trade Union) were given permission to start functioning as early as May 1945. Walter Ulbricht and the Soviet military administrators made sure that German personnel directors at all levels were KPD members who had lived and served in the Soviet Union during the war. On July 14, 1945, Ulbricht and Marshall Georgii Zhukov, the head of the Soviet Military Government, set up eleven central organisations to manage the governance of the Soviet zone and potentially serve as the basis for an all-German administration.[111] In early 1946 Stalin called Ulbricht to Moscow and instructed him to form a unity party before May Day. Meanwhile, Vasili Sokolovsky, the new Soviet occupation commander, pushed the SPD (Socialist Party of Germany) towards a union with the KPD (Communist Party of Germany) by means of deportations, arrests, imprisonment or death. The merger was created on April 21-22, 1946 with KPD members taking full and direct control of the SED (Socialist Unity Party).[112] At the beginning of 1947 the occupation authorities constituted the Administration of Internal Affairs and by the end of the year they announced the formation of a 'People's Police', with the view to establish the 'democratic means of crushing secret reactionary elements'.[113] By 1948 the SED dominated the political life of the Soviet zone to an extent that was out of proportion to its size and strength. Members of the SED occupied the greatest majority of positions in the central administration, and the most important posts in the provincial government structures.[114]

[111] Smyser, W. R., *From Yalta to Berlin*, p. 33.
[112] *Ibidem*, pp. 36-7.
[113] Nettl, J.P., *Eastern Zone and Soviet Policy in Germany 1945-50*, pp. 125-7.
[114] *Ibidem*, pp. 105-6.

The occupation authorities were keen to create a socio-economic system in the Eastern zone which would operate under the premises of the Communist credo. The Soviet military authorities in charge of the occupation acted with remarkable speed in order to achieve the economic rehabilitation of the Eastern zone. On January 15, 1947 the Central Secretariat of the SED announced the decision of the occupation authorities to curtail rationing, terminate industrial dismantling and transform two hundred industries originally earmarked to be converted into Soviet joint stock companies (*Sowjet-Aktiengesellschaften*), with 74 of those returning to the Land governments. Other measures included the reduction of quotas for reparations in kind and for more raw materials and tools to be placed at the disposal of farmers, artisans and small tradesmen. The Soviet authorities wanted the production level in the Eastern zone to be 2-3 times higher than that envisaged by the Allied Control Council (ACC) level of industry plan of March 1946.[115] Sokolovsky also gave the SED a greater role in the administration of the Soviet zone by devolving some of the authority held by the Soviets. On June 4, 1947, he ordered the establishment of the German Economic Council (DWK) under SED control as the civilian administration for the Soviet zone. Ulbricht used the DWK to complete SED control over the civilian administration of the Soviet zone. Ulbricht intended to use the DWK to replace the Soviet authorities and establish a separate East German civilian administration.[116] By 1948, the share of private industry had shrunk to 39% of the total industrial production and the state-owned trading organisation established by the newly-appointed German Economic Commission rapidly gained control of trading activities. The land reform of the early post-war period gave way to the beginning of collectivisation and the central command of the economy, established with the Two Year Plan 1949-50.[117]

[115] Communiqué issued by the SED, January 11, 1947 in Von Oppen, B., (ed), *Documents of Germany under Occupation 1945-1954*, pp. 202-3.
[116] Smyser, W. R.,, *From Yalta to Berlin*, p. 37.
[117] Berghahn., V. R., *Modern Germany: society, economy and politics in the twentieth century*, pp. 196-7.

The Soviet input in the polarisation process had a distinct revolutionist trait. By sovietising the Eastern zone, the Soviets created the basis for the political rehabilitation of the German territory under their command. Moreover, by linking sovietisation in Germany to the creation of a sphere of influence in Eastern Europe, the Soviets ensured the configuration of a permanent foothold in Germany and the integration of the Eastern zone into the nascent Communist bloc. This would significantly contribute to the creation of a bipolar situation in the international political system, in which Germany would lack the capabilities or the inclination to seek the destruction of the society of states.

The merging of the American and British zones of occupation, implemented on January 1, 1947, represented another important milestone in the path towards the partition of Germany and Europe. The evolution toward Bizonia stemmed from the 'grand design' scheme of a free-market international economic system, as envisaged by influential elements in the American establishment. This 'grand design' involved the reconstitution of Germany as the engine of a liberal economic system in Europe, capable of absorbing US capital and goods and preventing a return to an economic autarkic system in Europe.[118] Although the ACC kept operating and passing legislation affecting the whole of occupied Germany, Bizonia effectively put an end to the possibility of four power control and economic unity under a central government and set the tone for the division of Europe into two ideologically orientated blocs.

The diplomatic stalemate of the Moscow CFM of 1947 precipitated the partition of Germany. A revised plan for level of industry in Bizonia became operational on August 29, 1947. The revised plan provided for the retention of an industrial capacity approximate to 'the level of industry prevailing in Germany in 1936'. The plan established that the bizonal area had to be prepared

[118] The influence of the Council on Foreign Relations (CFR) in the post-war thinking of the State Department, particularly in regards to the rehabilitation of Germany, is well documented. The 'grand design' consisted in the creation of an international system which would provide an 'elbow room' for the development of the US economy along free-market lines. See Shoup, L. and Minter, W., *Imperial Brain Trust-The Council on Foreign Relations and the United States Foreign Policy* and Smith, N., *American Empire: Roosevelt's Geographer and the Prelude to Globalization.*

to exchange [...] proportionately larger quantities of industrial products in return for necessary food and raw material imports.[119]

The establishment of Bizonia brought the French into a trizonal agreement for the Western zones. The Coal Conference at Washington in August 1947 had recommended the transfer of coal production to German hands and supply to Western Europe. On August 22-27, 1947 British, American and French Governments representatives met in London to discuss matters relating to the level of industry in Bizonia and the management and control of the Ruhr mines and German economic resources. On November 19, 1947, the three governments established a bipartite coal control group and a German coal management board.[120]

In a politically orientated move, in January 1948 Clay and Robertson (the British military governor) summoned the German Minister Presidents and leaders of Bizonal Economic Council. The two governors recommended the doubling of the size of the Economic Council, the creation of a second chamber (made up of representatives of *Länder*), a new Executive Committee under a single Chair, the formation of a High Court, the development of a central bank and the fiscal reorganisation of Bizonia.[121] The Bizonal Economic Council established a Department of the Bizonal Economic Administrations to deal with matters including the 'problems of finance and subsidies connected with the coal industry as may concern the Economic Council', 'labour matters in the coal industry which are the concern of the Economic Council' and 'local allocations within the Bizonal area'. A German Coal Management (*Deutsche Bergbau Leitung*) was set up in Essen, becoming responsible for the direction of production and distribution of coal.[122]

[119] 'Revised Plan for the Level of Industry in the Bizonia,' August 29, 1947 in Von Oppen, B., Op. Cit., pp. 239-45.
[120] Communiqué on discussions between representatives of the United Kingdom, the United States and France in London, August 28, 1947 in Von Oppen, B., Op. Cit., pp. 238-9.
[121] Eisenberg, C.W., *Drawing the line: the American decision to divide Germany, 1944-1949*, p. 366.
[122] From the Anglo-American Announcement of the establishment of the Bipartite Coal Control Group and the German Coal Management Board in Von Oppen, B., Op. Cit., pp. 259-60.

On February 9, 1948 the Bizonal Economic Administration was reconstituted, now consisting of an Economic Council, a Länderrat, an Executive Committee and certain additional agencies. The Economic Council had the powers to adopt and enact ordinances on the administration of railways, maritime ports and coastal shipping, inland water transport, inter-Land inland waterways, intellectual property, communications and postal services, customs and the management of the Bizonal Civil Service. The Länderrat was composed of two representatives from each Land and was put in charge of legislation on matters within the competence of the Economic Council other than in respect of taxation or the appropriation of funds. The Executive Committee would be in charge of the administration of their respective functions, including the issue of implementing regulations under existing and future Bizonal legislation.[123] Also on February 9, 1948, a German High Court for the Combined Economic Area (*Obergericht für das vereinigte Wirtschaftsgebiet*) was established in Cologne.[124] The final decisive act towards partition was provided by the currency reform introduced in the Western zones on 20 June 1948 with the Deutsche Mark replacing the Reichsmark at one tenth of the value of the currency circulating in the Western Zones at the time, a move replicated by the Soviet Union in the Eastern zone.[125]

The failure of the Allies to agree on common guidelines for a united Germany at the Moscow and London CFM in 1947 prompted Washington to proceed with plans to rehabilitate the Western zones and create a political foothold via the Marshall Plan and the consolidation of a Western European political and military bloc. In a simultaneous approach, the Soviet Union consolidated its own bloc by sovietising the Eastern zone and solidifying the rapprochement between the Eastern European countries and Moscow.

[123] British Military Government Ordinance no.126, February 9, 1948 in Von Oppen, B., Op. Cit., pp. 268-75.
[124] British Military Government Ordinance no. 127, February 9, 1948 in Von Oppen, B., Op. Cit., pp. 275-79.
[125] British Military Government Law no.61, June 20, 1948 in Von Oppen, B., Op. Cit., pp. 292-4.

However, the clash of ideologies did not prevent the emergence of an international order capable of accommodating the two blocs. The United States and its Allies found it impossible to isolate the Soviet bloc from the post-war international order because of the increased level of institutionalisation of international society, the management of the spheres of influence system and their ongoing interest over the German Question. The polarisation of the post-war international society created during the occupation of Germany was achieved through an unprecedented level of great power interventionism, which was tempered by the existence of an international political system based on the tolerance for the diversity of interests. The common interests of the superpowers in successfully managing their respective spheres of influence entailed that both the Soviet Union and the Western bloc shared the civilisational requirements necessary for coexistence.[126]

Interventionism, informed by the ideological pursuit of the national interest, unfolded within the framework of coexistence. The superpowers proceeded to apply this modus operandi in their zones of occupation in Germany and ultimately in their spheres of influence. The interaction of conflict, cooperation and legality in the evolution towards German partition provided the superpowers with an example that would inform their actions during the next 40 years: *ideologically-driven competition would not lead to a situation of hot conflict.* The confrontation over Germany informed ideological competition in the post-war international order. The Cold War seldom, if ever, got hot enough to disrupt an international order beneficial to the superpowers.

[126] Gong argues that the concept of standard of 'civilisation' remains an integral part of international society. He defines this standard as the state in which a 'civilised' constituent of international society guarantees basic rights, exists as an organised political bureaucracy, has some self-defence capacity and adheres to general principles of international law and the international system. See Gong, G., *The Standard of 'Civilization' in International Society*, pp. 14-5.

VIII The Denazification of Germany

The Nazi period in Germany represented a cataclysm which engulfed the whole international political system. Nazism revolved around the concept of the *Volk* as a political idea which superseded that of the State. Hitler had peculiar ideas as to what constituted a *Volk*.[127] He understood the German Volk not as a Race, but as a medley of 'racial kernels'.[128] Hitler's dream of a master race (*Herrenvolk*) dominated his geopolitical vision. The conduct of Germany during the war derived to a considerable extent from the Führer's racialist thought. Racialism was not restricted to Nazi Germany. The United States and Britain had the experience of an Empire based on racial exceptionalism. Both nations had fought the war with segregated armies.

[127] The background of Hitler's anti-Jewish stance is abundantly documented. In his letter to Herr Gemlich of September 16, 1919 he states that 'Rational anti-semitism...must lead to a systematic and legal struggle against, and eradication of, the privileges the Jews enjoy over the other foreigners living among us (Alien Laws). Its final objective, however, must be the total removal of all Jews from our midst'. Point 4 of the Programme of the NSDAP, drafted by Hitler, and Anton Drexler on February 24, 1920 stated that 'only members of the nation may be citizens of the State. Only those of German blood, whatever their creed, may be members of the nation. Accordingly, no Jew may be a member of the nation'. In his *Political Testament* he states that 'It is untrue that I or anyone else in Germany wanted war in 1939. It was wanted and provoked solely by international statesmen either of Jewish origin or working for Jewish interests'. These documents were accessed at www.hitler.org.

[128] Lukacs, J., *The Hitler of History-Hitler's Biographers on Trial*, p. 123.

Nevertheless, Nazism was informed by race to the extent of making it impossible to achieve political accommodation with the national communities conquered through the campaign in the Eastern Front or to work together with them on a legal and diplomatic framework for the creation of a Nazi-orientated post-war international order.

The assault on the international order by the Nazi regime was informed by a strong racialist view. Racialism served to justify the search for geographical space and the constitution of an autarkic economic area. Fischer points out that according to Hitler, the German Volk had to reproduce itself more rapidly than the 'lesser races'. This required vital space *(Lebensraum)*.[129] During the 1930s Nazi Germany had marched into the demilitarised Rhineland, occupied by French forces, and embarked on an irredentist crusade by invading Austria, the Sudetenland and Czechoslovakia, before launching a war of aggression in Western and Eastern Europe. In previous chapters I have outlined the possible implications of an autarkic economic system in Europe and its perils for the United States and the British Empire. Although American private interests contributed to the buttressing of the Nazi war economy in the 1930s, the long term interests of the Allies would have been severely affected by the continuation of the Third Reich. Denazification in this context meant ridding Germany of its irredentist and challenging nature in order to secure a non-disruptive post-war international order.

The denazification of Germany entailed the creation of an environment conducive to securing the long range interests of the superpowers. These interests, while divergent from an economic perspective, found common ground on political aspects. Germany had to be subordinated politically for the enforcement of the 'grand design' schemes that the United States and the Soviet Union had in mind for the post-war international order. The superpowers achieved a discontinuity of Nazism by applying interventionist elements. This process unfolded within the diplomatic and legal framework that sustained the wartime alliance. It was due to this modus operandi that the transformation of

[129] Fischer, K., *Storia della Germania Nazista-Nascita e decandenza del Terzo Reich*, pp. 454-5.

Germany through denazification was successfully implemented and impacted positively on the post-war international order. The common aim of the Allies was to eliminate the Nazi ideology in order to prevent the disruptive resurgence of a politically independent Germany. According to Leffler, there were close similarities between Soviet and US policy regarding Germany. For the United States, a unified Germany was only imaginable if it were to be integrated into the Western system. A neutralised Germany, exposed to Soviet influence, was unthinkable in 1945 because the reconstruction of Europe, one of America's prominent aims, depended on access to the German market and raw materials. Soviet policy rested on the vision that a united Germany could only be possible if the Soviet Union maintained a decisive influence through the issue of reparations, co-determination of Ruhr affairs and Communist representation in all institutions.[130]

Discontinuity with Nazism would ensure that Germany would be rid of the ideology that subverted the international order since the 1930s. The process of denazification was geared towards eliminating Nazism as a legitimate political movement and as a doctrine representing the aspirations of Germany in the international order.

The reformation of the German political system was an issue that the Allies fully agreed on since the Declaration of Unconditional Surrender at Casablanca in 1943. At Yalta, the Allies decided to provide safeguards against a potential military revival of Germany, to eradicate German militarism and the Nazi general staff, to bring about the denazification of Germany, to punish the war criminals and to disarm and demilitarise Germany.[131] The provisions agreed upon at Potsdam implied great changes in German society as well as its political system. The number of Germans who belonged to the Nazi Party had reached 13 million by the end of the war. Resistance to Hitlerism lacked concrete support. Unlike 1918, when the Russians hoped for a revolution in Germany and the Entente Powers acted in defence of German society as they

[130] Leffler, M., *The Struggle for Germany and the Origins of the Cold War*, pp. 5-6.
[131] Proektor, D., 'The Yalta Conference and the German Problem' in Iakovlev, A. N., *The Yalta Conference 1945: lessons of history*, p. 129.

had found it,[132] the superpowers agreed on the need to bring about profound changes in German society. The Potsdam Agreement called for

> the complete disarmament and demilitarisation of Germany and the elimination or control of all German industry that could be used for military production...[the destruction of the] National Socialist Party and its affiliated and supervised organisations' and 'the eventual reconstruction of German political life.[133]

The legal framework established during the war stated the unanimous and unambiguous will of the Allies to reform what they perceived as the militaristic, warlike disposition of Germany, and its potential to disrupt the international political system. It was in the Allies' interest to demilitarise the character of German society and make it receptive to the kind of international order desired by the superpowers. The Western Allies achieved this aim by setting up political and economic foundations akin to liberal democracy and free market economics. The Soviets accomplished the objective of denazifying Germany by implementing socialistic measures that were directed against the big landowners and captains of industry who supported Hitler's rise to power and its war of aggression on the international order.

The first instrument of denazification was the work done by the ACC. The ACC was responsible for the passage of measures that facilitated the denazification of German society. On September, 20 1945 the ACC abolished 'all German land, naval and air forces, the SS, SA, SD, Gestapo... and associations which serve to keep alive the military tradition in Germany'. Furthermore, the proclamation established that the National Socialist German Workers' Party (NSDAP) would be 'abolished and declared to be illegal'.[134] On October 10, 1945 the ACC liquidated the 'National Socialist German

[132] Davidson, B., *Germany: What Now ?- Potsdam 1945-Partition 1949*, pp. 19-20.
[133] Section II (a), Protocol of the Proceedings-Postdam Conference, August 1, 1945-http://www.yale.edu/lawweb/avalon/decade/decade17.htm.
[134] Control Council proclamation no. 2: certain additional requirements imposed on Germany, September 20, 1945-From Von Oppen, B., Op. Cit., pp. 68-79.

Labour Party, its formations, affiliated associations and supervised agencies, including paramilitary organisations and all other Nazi institutions established as instruments of party domination'.[135] ACC Proclamation no. 3 of October 20, 1945 established the fundamental principles of judicial reform, stipulating equality before the law, regardless of 'race, nationality or religion', that 'no person shall be deprived of life, liberty or property without due process of law', the liquidation of the extraordinary Hitler Courts and the independence of the judiciary. Law no. 4 provided for the reorganisation of the German judicial system. This reorganisation included the reintroduction of the Weimar legal system and the dismissal of judges and prosecutors who had taken part in the punitive practices of the Hitlerite regime.[136] The Allies agreed on the elimination and prohibition of military training on November 30, 1945 as well as 'all military educational institutions'.[137] On December 20, 1945, the ACC established the guidelines to be applied for the punishment of people guilty of war crimes. In the same vein, the ACC Directive no. 24 of January 12, 1946 ordered the removal from office and from positions of responsibility of Nazis and persons hostile to Allied purposes. Persons were to be treated as

> more than nominal participants in Party Activities...[and as] hostile to Allied purposes...[in cases when they] authorised or participated affirmatively in any Nazi crimes, racial persecutions or discriminations...been avowed believers in Nazism or racial and militaristic creeds...[or] voluntarily given substantial moral or material support or political assistance of any kind to the Nazi Party or Nazi officials and leaders.[138]

ACC Directive no. 32 of June 26, 1946 stated that any

[135] Control Council Law no.2: Providing for the termination and liquidation of the Nazi organizations, October 10, 1945-From Von Oppen, B., Op. Cit., pp. 79-81.
[136] Control Council Proclamation no. 3: Fundamental principles of judicial reform, October 10, 1945-From Von Oppen, B., Op. Cit., pp. 81-2.
[137] Control Council Law no. 8: Elimination and prohibition of military training, November 30, 1945-From Von Oppen, B., Op. Cit., pp. 90-3.
[138] Control Council Law no. 10: Punishment of persons guilty of war crimes, crimes against peace and against humanity, December 20, 1945-From Von Oppen, B., Op. Cit., pp. 97-107.

> member of the administrative or teaching staff of any educational institution who in any way whatsoever spreads or assists in spreading or connives at spreading militaristic, Nazi or anti-democratic doctrines will be dismissed from such institutions.

ACC Directive no. 38 ordered the arrest and punishment of war criminals, Nazis and militarists, and the internment, control and surveillance of potentially dangerous Germans, with explicit reference to the Potsdam Agreement and supplementary ACC directives.[139] On February 25, 1947 ACC Law no. 46 abolished the State of Prussia, a decision confirmed during the Moscow CFM in 1947. The Allies agreed that the symbolism enshrined in the survival of the Prussian state had no place in a reconstituted Germany. The British representative in the ACC stated that

> The survival of the Prussian state...would provide the basis for any irredentist claims which the German people may later seek to put forward, would strengthen the German militarist ambitions, and would encourage the revival of the authoritarian, centralised Germany.[140]

Directive no. 54 of 25 June 1947 established the basic Principles for the Democratisation of Education in Germany, which included 'equal education opportunity for all' and free of charge provision of 'tuition, textbooks and other necessary scholastic material...for pupils of compulsory school age'. This assistance was extended to pupils of other educational institutions, including universities. The directive also established that

> compulsory full-time school attendance should be required for all [children] between the ages of six and at least fifteen.

[139] Control Council Directive no. 32: Disciplinary measures against managing and administrative staffs of educational institutions, teaching staff, and students guilty of militaristic, nazi, or anti-democratic propaganda, June 26, 1946-From Von Oppen, B., Op. Cit., p. 142.
[140] ACC Coordinating Committee-Abolition of the State of Prussia-Memorandum of the British member, August 8, 1946-FO 631/2454, p. 1.

It also set the foundations for a clear path to tertiary education, emphasising the need for

> education for civic responsibility and a democratic way of life...[and] understanding of and respect for other nations.[141]

The work of the ACC was undertaken within a strong liberal framework.[142] The passing and enforcement of legislation outlawing Nazism from German political life would have a transformative effect on the post-war international order as both the Federal and Democratic German republics adopted similar measures in regards to the safeguard of basic civil liberties.[143] Moreover, the two Germanys adopted a bandwagoning position vis-à-vis the superpowers rather than reconstructing themselves as revisionist forces. This position would entail that up until the 1970s, changes in the status quo leading up to the rapprochement between the two Germanys were discussed in adherence to the rules established by the occupying powers.

The second instrument of denazification was the work done at zonal level by the Allies on educational and cultural reform and the implementation of the denazification tribunals. The need to accomplish a discontinuity with Nazism propelled the Allies to ensure that the occupied country would be rid of the ideology that subverted the international political system since the 1930s.

US policy on educational and cultural reform evolved from re-education to reorientation. Reorientation brought with it a new emphasis to end denazification. At the same time, the American occupation authorities established cultural and

[141] From ACC Directive no. 54, June 25, 1947- Von Oppen, B., Op. Cit., pp. 233-4.

[142] Kant states that 'the only constitution...on which all juridical legislation of a people must be based, is the republican. This constitution is established, firstly, by principles of the freedom of the members of a society (as men); secondly, by principles of dependence of all upon a single common legislation (as subjects); and, thirdly, by the law of their equality (as citizens).' See Kant, I., *Perpetual Peace: A Philosophical Sketch*, section 2-http://www.mtholyoke.edu/acad/intrel/kant/kant1.htm.

[143] The Constitution of the Democratic Republic of Germany provided for the protection of the 'inalienable rights to its citizens' (articles 6-49). The Constitution of the Federal Republic of Germy included similar provisions (Articles 1-21).

educational interchange networks and reopened the Free University of Berlin. There are a number of important measures which aided this process of reorientation. SWNCC 269/8, which received official acceptance on October 24, 1946, permitted the exchange of persons between Germany and the United States. In February 1947 SWNCC 269/10 was issued in order to regulate the interchange of cultural and educational material between the two countries. In July 1947 it was modified by SWNCC 269/11, to allow exchange between Germans in the US Zone with other countries.[144]

Re-education was undertaken with the view to prevent a recurrence of aggression rather than to remould the German consciousness.[145] Cultural reform was undertaken through the broadcasting of the American way of life in Youth Centres and the *Amerika Haus* network, also known as US Information Centres.[146] The Psychological Warfare Division of SHAEF and the Information Control Division of the US Zone of occupation resorted to informational and educational means such as the press, radio, books, pictures, schools and the churches.[147] Willett opines that re-education was not as potent as the method of

> ideological reproduction taking place as a consequence of the free market economy, and the unrestricted operation of American business and the mass media.[148]

The Education Branch of the US Zone was pivotal in restoring school buildings, selecting educators and textbooks, and removing Nazis from the teaching staff. By the end of 1945 1,849,206 children were in school. A revival of pre-1933 youth organisations took place. As rapidly as faculty staff were screened, high schools and universities, which received US technical assistance, were built.[149]

[144] Trent, J., *Mission on the Rhine,* p. 258.
[145] Willett, R., *The Americanization of Germany 1945-1949*, p. 16.
[146] *Ibidem*, pp. 17-20.
[147] Clay, L., *Decision in Germany*, pp. 281-2.
[148] Willett, R., *The Americanization of Germany 1945-1949*, p. 27.
[149] Clay, L., *Decision in Germany*, p. 299.

On July 1945 the US occupation authorities licensed the first German newspaper, the *Frankfurter Rundschau*, with a circulation of 741,500, published three times a week by refugees of the Hitler regime. During 1945, information libraries were created in Frankfurt, Munich and Berlin, supplying the German people with books and periodicals and portraying the American way of life. In October 1946 DANA (later renamed DENA), the news service of the American zone, was created by the Military Government and modelled by Associated Press. In April 1946 a second newspaper was licensed in Frankfurt, re-establishing a competitive press in the US Zone for the first time.[150]

The US Zone issued a denazification directive on July 7, 1945 establishing that all high-level civil servants who joined the Nazi party before May 1, 1937 were to be removed from office. In addition, the Handbook for the Military Government in Germany contained a list of 136 'mandatory removal and exclusion categories'. OMGUS Law no. 8 issued on September 6, 1945 and ACC Directive no. 24 of January 12, 1946, signed by all four Allied powers, expanded the categories of persons subject to the denazification program.[151]

In August 1945, the US Military governor granted an amnesty from all denazification proceedings to persons born after January 1, 1919. On November 5, 1945, during the fourteenth meeting of the Länderrat in Sttutgart, Clay expressed his satisfaction with the German denazification tribunals. On Christmas Day, an amnesty was granted to all those with incomes of less than RM 3,600 during the Nazi era and taxable property valued below RM 20,000.[152]

The Law for Liberation from National Socialism and Militarism was finally passed on March 5, 1946, in response to the need to expedite matter in the context of the new political realities of the nascent international order. The law established a distinction between major and minor offenders, followers and those exonerated. All persons over the age of eighteen were required to fill out questionnaires (*Fragebogen*) to determine their classification. Five hundred and forthy-five tribunals (*Spruchkammer*) and appeal courts employing 22,000

[150] *Ibidem*, pp. 282-4.
[151] Merrit, *Democracy Imposed*, pp. 181-2.
[152] *Ibidem*, p. 183.

people implemented these directives. On July 11, 1947, JCS directive 1779 took effect, marking a change in US policy on Germany. US policy goals thus shifted from a punitive occupation of Germany to a 'more liberal' policy, allowing the occupied zone to create 'a self-sustaining economy' and providing Germans with the opportunity to express greater political initiative. The amendment of JCS 1067 meant that denazification had to be terminated, as German cooperation was needed in order to implement the ERP. In October 1947 OMGUS asked the German Länder to amend the Law for Liberation from National Socialism and Militarism for the sake of accomplishing a more expeditious treatment of the subject.[153] The Länderrat passed a new amendment on March 25, 1948. OMGUS reported 28,065 'hard-core' cases to be tried but amendments pushed the issue to the margins.[154]

The aims of British occupational policy in Germany were to induce 'responsible government, federation of Germany and European partnership' and for Germany never to be able to launch another war of aggression. The initial aims of the military government were for re-education to go hand in hand with the prevention of an economic collapse, and the de-prussianisation of Germany.[155] Marshall argues that the British approach to the occupation was 'technical' rather than political when it came to the establishment of political life. The occupation authorities did not believe in democracy from the bottom upwards without political content.[156]

The British approach to educational reform was to seek early personal contacts with German teachers and to encourage exchange programmes. Like the US occupation authorities, Britain attempted to restrict church control over schools, to expand primary education and to oppose any reintroduction of school fees. Their efforts were largely unsuccessful, since the reactionary elements within their zones soon gained political influence in the shape of the

[153] Eisenberg, C.W., *Drawing the line: the American decision to divide Germany, 1944-1949*, p. 373.
[154] *Ibidem*, p. 374.
[155] Turner, I. (Ed.), *Reconstruction in Post-War Germany*, pp. 4-6.
[156] Marshall, B., *The Origins of Post-War German Politics*, pp. 198-200.

newly founded Christian Democratic Union (CDU).[157] At the beginning, teachers were dismissed in the most obvious cases of Nazi affiliation.[158] A British report on 'German Textbook Literature' describes how every effort was made to eliminate nationalism, racism, militarism, violence and cruelty, as well as hostility towards international world organisations reminiscent of attitudes prevalent in the Wilhelmine period.[159]

By the late 1946 the British authorities had used the categorisation process as a means to rehabilitate many of the less serious offenders.[160] The British employed a 'legal' approach towards denazification and refused to cooperate with German anti-fascist organisations. The British denazification panels functioned under the advisement of German anti-Nazis. On October 1, 1947 the British Military Government decreed that the Land governments would be in charge of the denazification process. The Land administrations were also given the right to 'alter or revoke existing zonal instruction'.[161] Demotions occurred until 1948-9, when many former offenders climbed back towards their old positions.[162] Turner argues that the greatest impact of denazification in the British zone was amongst the political elites, with the civil service being less affected and the industrial elite barely touched.[163]

In the French zone, the military commanders gave the people responsible for the different aspects of the occupation a large degree of autonomy. The Director of Education, Raymond Schmittlein, a Germanist by profession, defined the goals of the occupation as to

> free the German youth of the yoke of discipline which kills his judgement, the Wagnerian nightmares that poison its imagination...to make her understand that

[157] Hahn, H.J., *Education and Society in Germany*, p. 95.
[158] Samuel R., and Thomas R., *Education and Society in Modern Germany*, p.175.
[159] Davis, K. S., 'The Problem of Textbooks', in Hearnden (ed.), *The British in Germany*, p. 115.
[160] Turner, I., 'Denazification in the British Zone' in Turner, I. (ed), *Reconstruction in Post-War Germany-British Occupation Policy and the Western Zones, 1945-55*, p. 239.
[161] British Military Government Ordinance no.110, October 1, 1947- Von Oppen, B., Op. Cit., pp. 247-50.
[162] Ebsworth, R., *Restoring Democracy in Germany-The British Contribution*, pp. 11-3.
[163] Turner, I., 'Denazification in the British Zone' in Turner, I. (ed), Op. Cit., p. 266.

nationalism was imposed on her artificially... [and] to show her that the philosophy of the 'Superman'...can only lead to catastrophe.[164]

The French employed the American concept of re-education. Re-education had the purpose of bringing about a change in the political and institutional mindset.[165] Textbooks issued in the French zone downplayed the Prussian influence on the history of Germany, stressing instead the ties that bound Germany with the rest of Europe, especially France. They also depicted Prussia as a reactionary power which thwarted the effects of the Enlightenment and the French Revolution.[166] Denazification was stringent in the teaching profession, with less than 50% of elementary and secondary teachers being retained. Notably though, a much less severe process was implemented in the field of industry.[167]

Although the educational and cultural reform faced resistance from local circles, education policy in the French zone was very comprehensive. The occupation authorities had the aims of reforming the teaching profession, publishing new textbooks and reforming the secondary and higher education systems.[168] The occupation authorities created nine teaching schools in Rhineland-Pfalz and Baden-Württemberg, which in 1947 provided 500 teachers to the education system.[169] Educational reform began in primary schools, which reopened in September 1945. Sixteen teacher-training colleges patterned after the French *écoles normales* were founded. All textbooks published after 1933 were banned. By 1947, the French zone published more

[164] Ruge-Schatz, A., 'Le Revers de la médaille-Contradictions et limites de l'apport culturel du government militarire français en Allemagne' in Vaillant, J. (ed.), *La Denazification par les Vainqueurs-La Politique Culturelle des Occupants en Allemagne 1945-1949*, p. 107.
[165] *Ibidem, 1945-1949*, p. 106.
[166] For a close examination of the aspects involving re-education in the Western zones see Torriani, R., *Nazis into Germans: Re-education and democratisation in the British and French Zones of Occupation, 1945-1949* - PhD Thesis (Cambrdige) (2005).
[167] Willis, F.R., *France, Germany and the New Europe, 1945-1963*, pp. 42-3.
[168] Ruge-Schatz, A., 'Le Revers de la médaille-Contradictions et limites de l'apport culturel du government militarire français en Allemagne' in Vaillant, J. (ed.), Op. Cit., p. 108.
[169] Guth, S., *Les Forces Françaises en Allemagne-La Citadelle Utopique*, pp. 29-30.

textbooks per child than the British and American zones.[170] Secondary education was reformed in June 1946. Reform included the unification of schools, the mixing of boys and girls and more choice in regards to the curriculum.[171] French culture and history were taught in French, as were teacher-training courses. German culture was de-emphasised and American textbooks were kept out of the French Zone.[172] The *Abitur* (secondary education leaving certificate) system was modeled on the French *baccalauréat*, introducing a clearly defined path from secondary to higher education.[173] As for the university system, the French introduced curriculum reform and reopened the universities of Tübingen and Freiburg. Libraries were provided with 1,340,650 'syllabaires' and books for primary education, 574,820 German classics, translations of French and English books, 868,280 dictionaries and manuals in French, 630,000 French literary texts and 240,000 history books.[174]

Cultural policy was actively pursued and served as a transformative element within the occupational structure as well as to mitigate the psychological impact of economic exploitation.[175] The absence of coordination between the military administration in Baden-Baden and at Land and Kreis level created the conditions for several cultural initiatives in the zone. Cultural activity was revitalised through theatre and cinema, with performances by French actors in Baden. The old University of Mainz was reopened. The *École d'Administration* in Spire, the Institute of Translators in Gemersheim and a number of pedagogic academies were set up in order to root the French influence.[176] The Institute of European History at Mainz was established and eight popular universities (*Volksuniversität*) were opened, offering evening

[170] Willis, F.R., *France, Germany and the New Europe, 1945-1963,* pp. 44-5.

[171] Ruge-Schatz, A., 'Le Revers de la médaille-Contradictions et limites de l'apport culturel du government militarire français en Allemagne' in Vaillant, J. (ed.), Op. Cit., p. 109.

[172] See Zauner, S., *Erziehung und Kulturmission: Frankreichs Bildungs-Politik in Deutschland,* 1945-1949.

[173] Guth, S., *Les Forces Françaises en Allemagne-La Citadelle Utopique,* pp. 31-2.

[174] *Ibidem,* pp. 32-3.

[175] Willis, F.R., *France, Germany and the New Europe, 1945-1963,* p. 46.

[176] Moreau, J., 'Les Aspects Particuliers de la Politique d'Occupation Française dans les domaines de la jeunesse et de l'education populaire' in Vaillant, J. (ed.), Op. Cit., p. 21.

instruction and college degrees.[177]

France revitalised the press and on September 8, 1945 *Südkurier*, the first approved newspaper was published. The press introduced the subject of denazification and grouped all anti-Nazi organisations (Antifa groups) like *Das Neue Deutschland.*[178] There was a revitalisation of pre-Hitler youth movements such as *Bund der Katholischen Jugend, Evangelische Jugend* and *Naturfreunde.*[179] There was an assiduous Franco-German cultural collaboration at the level of youth organisations like the *Peuple et Culture* movement, the *Centre d'Echanges Internationaux* and *Service Jeunesse et Education Populaire.*[180] French teachers (*Lecteurs d'education populaire*) taught in the popular schools (*Volkshochschulen)*, portraying France's social and cultural values.[181]

In the French zone, the denazification process entailed not just the removal of former Nazis from the civil service but also administrative reform.[182] A General Directorate of Justice under Charles Furby was put in charge of judicial reform. Separate courts were created in each Land as well as a High Court in Rastatt.[183] German Denazification Committees were set up by the French First Army and the military government and a purge of those holding office was well under way in October 1945.[184] By 1946 each Land in the French zone had developed its own denazification system, with Württemberg having the most efficient of them all. Nevertheless, denazification was not given a high priority by the occupation authorities as it was seen to have little political utility. As France's main interest in the occupation of Germany was of

[177] Willis, F.R., *France, Germany and the New Europe, 1945-1963,* pp. 4-5.
[178] Ferber, G., 'Vicissitudes ou les débuts de la presse à Constance en 1945-1946' in Vaillant, J. (ed.), Op. Cit., pp. 78-9.
[179] Moreau, J., *Les Aspects Particuliers de la Politique d'Occupation Française dans les domaines de la jeunesse et de l'education populaire*, p. 27.
[180] *Ibidem*, pp. 24-5.
[181] *Ibidem*, p. 29.
[182] Hillel, M, *L'Occupation Francaise en Allemagne,* pp. 160-2.
[183] Willis, F.R., *The French in Germany 1945-9,* pp. 153-4.
[184] *Ibidem*, p. 155.

an economic nature, any approach to denazification that conflicted with that aim had little chance of being adopted.

In the Eastern zone, educational and cultural reform was intended to foster peaceful cooperation among nations. The September 1, 1946 the law of democratisation of German schools introduced twelve years of compulsory education as well as state control of the educational system. Teaching courses were imbued with an emphasis on Marxist indoctrination and political 'progressiveness', while the selection of candidates was almost entirely in the hands of the SED.[185] The emphasis on cultural reform hinged upon the establishment of a 'popular front', accommodating people not necessarily associated with the SED, and the entrenchment of the anti-fascist struggle for the democratic renewal of Germany. Cultural and educational policy revolved around this notion, particularly under the chairmanship of Johannes R. Becher, a KPD Moscow exile during the war, and president of the Cultural Association for the Democratic Renewal of Germany from July 1945.[186] The antifascist education in the Eastern zone sought to unify the German nation in political terms and to create a cultural base akin to the socialist ideals. At the heart of these concepts was the uniform schooling of citizens in the *Einheitschule*, so as to erase the notion of class and confessional and gender divisions. Blessing argues that the antifascist education practiced in schools did not replicate the state ideology dictated by Moscow for controlling its satellites. The educational reformers consciously fostered the German nature of the reforms.[187] The Soviets integrated the school system with the socialist method of production. Seventh grade students had to work in factories one day a week. Those who

[185] Samuel R.H. and R. Hinton Thomas, *Education and Society in Modern Germany*, pp. 172-3.
[186] McCauley, M., *The German Democratic Republic since 1945*, p. 40-1. Johannes R. Becher became the first Minister of Culture of the GDR. His literary work is indicative of a trend that would carry on until the 1953 crisis and is concerned with the idea of communication with non-proletarian writing and keeping the channels open with the West. See Davies, P., 'Ein schönes, ungetrenntes Ganzes: Johannes R. Becher and the Kulturnation' in Flanagan, C., and Taberner, S., *1949/1989-Cultural Perspectives on Division and Unity in East and West.*
[187] Blessing, B., *The Antifascist classroom-Denazification in Soviet-occupied Germany, 1945-1949*, pp. 188-9.

refused or opposed Communism were not allowed to go to high school and had to undertake apprenticeships instead.[188]

In the Eastern Zone, denazification brought about the complete overhaul of the socio-economic system, with the purge of the social and economic elites from their pre-1945 positions. Whilst this was probably done in the hope that this policy would generate popular support amongst the rest of the population, the purges forced an exodus of East Germans into the Western zones. Communists or Social Democrats took up prominent positions in the civil service, local government, the education system and the judiciary.[189] Denazification tribunals were largely staffed and under the control of reliable SPD and KPD members. This extended to the appointment of Burgermeister, police chiefs and senior officials, all in charge of purging their departments.[190]

Order no. 201 of 16 August 1947 established the guidelines for the execution of ACC Directives no. 24 and 38 on denazification. Order no. 201 executed the confiscation of 'landed property of the Junkers, fascists, and war criminals' as well as credit and banking institutes, and private enterprises formerly belonging to active fascists and militarists. The Order also provided that

> former members of the Nazi party who have not themselves committed crimes against peace and against the security of other peoples or crimes against the German people [were] to be granted not only the right to vote, but also the right to stand for election.

The Order established that German administrative bodies and Denazification Commissions were to take the

[188] Behncke, M., *Democratization or Sovietization? The Development of the Soviet Zone of Occupation in Germany 1945-1950 in the light of recent findings* (PhD thesis, Pacific Western University, 1983), p. 77.
[189] Pritchard, G., *The Making of the GDR 1945-53-From Antifascism to Stalinism*, p. 86.
[190] *Ibidem*, pp. 83-4.

necessary measures for the acceleration of the execution and completion of denazification in the Soviet zone of occupation.[191]

On May 25, 1946 the Soviet Commanders nationalised the entire

property of the Nazi Party and its affiliated bodies and the works and enterprises of war criminals, leaders, and active protagonists of the Nazi Party and the Nazi state, as well as the works and enterprises which have actively served the crime of war.[192]

The implementation of cultural and educational reform varied in each of the occupation zones. However, the Allies had a common purpose: to transform Germany by achieving a discontinuity with Nazism. The process of cultural and educational reform as well as the implementation of denazification at zonal level had drawbacks on both sides of the Elbe. The Western Allies were eager to expedite the process of cultural and educational rehabilitation, and reinstate the captains of industry who had helped the rise of Hitler in order to accomplish their structural interests. The Soviet authorities in the Eastern zone implemented their cultural and educational reforms in order to bring about the sovietisation of the political system. The liberal aspects attached to the elements of transformation in Germany would create a reorientation of the mindset of ordinary Germans. However, Peterson argues that the major change was psychological and indigenous. Germany was in large part denazified by Hitler because Nazism was based on success and Hitler failed. Germans might have been more dissuaded from fascism and communism than persuaded to democracy,[193] as seen in the flight of the German soldiers and ordinary citizens towards the zones occupied by the Western armies upon the end of the war. Moreover, the imposition of Communist rule in the Eastern zone brought with

[191] ACC Order no. 201, August 16, 1947- *Documents on Germany under Occupation 1945-54*, pp. 234-6.
[192] Draft Law on the Transfer of the Enterprises of War Criminals and Nazi Criminals and Land Saxony, May 25, 1946-From *Documents on Germany under Occupation*, p. 136.
[193] Peterson, E.N., *The American Occupation of Germany*, pp. 341-2.

it the brutality of the Red Army towards civilians, particularly women, during the early stages of the occupation.

The most transformative outcome of the treatment of the German Question was the reconciliation between German aspirations in the international political system (particularly in the case of West Germany) and the structural interests of the superpowers. Since the unification of the German polity within the framework of the nation-state, the great European powers (particularly Britain and France) perceived Germany as a threat. As a latecomer to the imperial race and unified as a single state many centuries later than England and France, Germany was perceived as a challenger to the international order since the late nineteenth century. By the turn of the twentieth century Germany had become a mighty economic power, with the size of her economy surpassing that of France and achieving parity with that of Britain. Overseas investments grew exponentially. In 1914 the pursuit of *Weltpolitik* had caused a major disruption of the international order. The Nazi period magnified the potential threat of Germany. In 1945, Richter stated that the 'way of purification' should lie ahead in a European community of freedom, equality, and brotherhood which could inspire and control nations.[194] The surrender of the German state to the Allies in the aftermath of World War Two would produce a reorientation of the German political character towards Europeanisation. Undoubtedly, the work done by the Allies on denazification (understood as the reconstitution of the German political character) would be the main factor in this reorientation. The Allies succeeded in eradicating Nazism as a viable political alternative for Germany. Muhlen mentions that by the time of the 1952 elections, the nationwide conventions of the CDU, the SPD, the German Federation of Trade Unions as well as assemblies of university students, physicians, booksellers and book publishers representing millions of Germans assailed Nazism and pledged never to let it grow again.[195]

[194] Richter, W., *Re-educating Germany*, p. 214.
[195] Muhlen, N., *The Return of Germany-A Tale of Two Countries*, p. 5.

The third instrument in the denazification of Germany was the implementation of the International Military Tribunals (IMT). At Nuremberg, war crimes perpetrators and the main leaders of the Third Reich were tried by judges representing the four occupation powers. The unprecedented nature of the crimes committed in Nazi Germany, the dislocation and devastation caused by their revisionist challenge on the international political system and the level of interventionism of the superpowers in the realignment of the international political system prompted the trial of the ideology that disrupted the international order. Nuremberg had an antecedent in the Leipzig trials which took place after the end of World War One, when the Germans tried the Kaiser and other former soldiers and generals. However, the victors of the Great War did not press with extraditions and Wilhelm II was charged on moral and political grounds, not on crimes against humanity.[196]

The London Charter of the International Military Tribunal, drafted by Robert H. Jackson, Robert Falco, and Iona Nikitchenko, was established on August 8, 1945. The Charter set down the laws and procedures by which the Nuremberg trials were to be conducted. The Charter defined that only crimes committed by the European Axis could be tried. Three categories of crimes were defined: war crimes, crimes against peace, and crimes against humanity. The Charter also stated that the official's position was not a valid defense against war crime charges. Between October 18, 1945, and October 1, 1946, the (IMT) tried twenty-two 'major' war criminals on charges of conspiracy, crimes against peace, war crimes, and crimes against humanity.[197]

The IMT defined crimes against humanity as

> murder, extermination, enslavement, deportation...or persecutions on political, racial, or religious grounds.[198]

[196] Woetzel, R., *The Nuremberg Trials in Internationlal Law (with a postlude on the Eichmann case*, p. 35.
[197] For an account of the proceedings see Owen, J, *The Nuremberg Trials Evil on Trial.*
[198] London Charter, August 8, 1945- www.yale.edu/lawweb/avalon/imt/proc/imtchart.htm.

Twelve of those convicted were sentenced to death, amongst them Hans Frank, Hermann Göring, Alfred Rosenberg, and Julius Streicher, masterminders and executioners of the policies which stemmed from the ideology on trial.

Under the aegis of the IMT, American military tribunals conducted twelve further trials of high-ranking German officials at Nuremberg, referred to collectively as the Subsequent Nuremberg Proceedings. Gestapo and SS members, as well as German industrialists, were tried for their roles in implementing the Nuremberg Laws, 'Aryanisation', mass shootings of Jews in concentration camps, shootings by Einsatzgruppen (mobile killing units), deportations, forced labor, sale of Zyklon B, and medical experiments.

Nuremberg introduced a liberal concept of international law; namely, the principle that professional soldiers cannot escape punishment for waging aggressive wars and permitting crimes against humanity with the claim they were dutifully carrying out orders issued by their superiors. Nuremberg is an example of effective international law being implemented and, adding a clear interventionist dimension, of sovereignty and territoriality being by-passed as responsibility was devolved down to the individual.[199]

Persico argues that the legacy of Nuremberg, although contradictory, documented beyond question the atrocities committed by the Nazi regime and contributed to the creation of a democratic system in Germany, as the German population became fully aware of the worst aspects of Nazism.[200] Although Nuremberg could not root out all the elements involved with the Nazi regime, it contributed to the denazification of German society. The Nuremberg trials also provided the German people with a clean slate and solidified the process of discontinuity with Nazism. The Nuremberg trials were an eloquent example of the interventionist approach of the superpowers. Nuremberg would have a lasting transformative effect on the Cold War international order as it created an important interventionist precedent for situations involving the disruption of the international order and gross violation of human rights, as in the case of the

[199] Calvocoressi, P., *Nuremberg-The facts, the law and the consequences*, pp.118-9.
[200] Persico, J., *Nuremberg-Infamy on Trial*, p. 441.

former Yugoslavia and Rwanda in the 1990s and the trial of dictatorial leaders in South America.[201]

[201] Despite his release on grounds of ill health, the unprecedented detention of General Augusto Pinochet in the United Kingdom in 2000 for crimes against humanity committed in his own country, without a warrant or request for extradition from Chile, marks a watershed in international law. Some scholars consider it one of the most important events in judicial history since the Nuremberg trials of Nazi war criminals. Spanish judge Baltasar Garzón's case was largely founded on the principle of universal jurisdiction; that certain crimes are so egregious that they constitute crimes against humanity and can therefore be prosecuted in any court in the world. The British House of Lords ruled that Pinochet had no right to immunity from prosecution as a former head of state, and could be put on trial. This interventionist principle is undoubtedly one of the legacies of the work of the IMT during 1945-6.

VIII The Role of Intervention in the Post-war International Order

Intervention became a primary institution of the post-war international order because of the decisive input that the Allies had in achieving a bipolar solution for the German Question and the way that this affected the formation of spheres of influence. The policy of unconditional surrender, agreed upon by the Allies at the Casablanca Conference in January-February 1943, meant that the political future of Germany would be the pivotal element in the shaping of the post-war international society. The occupation of a defeated nation had little precedent in the modern history of the international political system. This kind of intervention indicated the commitment of the victors to transform Germany, and in the process, to a radically changed international order.[202] Although the Allies had different interests in regards to Germany, in order to attain them, they were compelled to maintain the ethical and functional cohabitation of the wartime years. A more integrated world and the emergence of two blocs meant the possibility of intervention like never before in international history.

The treatment of the German Question during the 1943-8 period produced a change of attitude reflected in the renewed dimension of the role of ethics in

[202] France was occupied by Alliance forces in 1815 in order to enforce the settlement imposed by the Congress of Vienna. See McGuigan, R, *The Allied Occupation Army In Post-Waterloo France*. Also, Veve, T. D., *The Duke of Wellington and the British Army of Occupation in France, 1815-1818*.

the international political system. The experience of the Nuremberg trials enshrined in international law the view that intervention was justified in the case of gross violation of human rights. International law was institutionalised through the creation of the United Nations organisation, the expansion of the concept of human rights, as well as the enlargement of the legitimacy and authority of international organisations and regimes.[203]

The Atlantic Charter of 1941 laid down the foundations for the political, military and economic involvement of the United States on a global scale. The Teheran Conference of 1943 consolidated a workable rapport between the Western Allies and the Soviet Union. The Yalta and Potsdam Conferences (1945) created the framework needed for the discussion of complex issues involved in the treatment of the German Question and the post-war international political system. The CFMs would become a useful instrument for the realignment of the post-war international order by acting as a forum for the discussion and implementation of the peace treaties with the former Axis powers. This legal and diplomatic machinery solidified the practical association framework during the war and contributed to shape the configuration of the post-war international order. The creation of the legal and diplomatic framework which established the post-war constitutional settlement responded to the need to address the German Question. It primarily responded to the need to win the war and ensure that the Allies would be bound together in a common framework of action for the purposes of delineating the post-war international order. After the war, international law ensured that the breakdown of the practical association would not result in a disruptive situation for the nascent international order.

Intervention as a primary institution of the post-war international order entailed the transformation of Germany from top to bottom. This approach differed from the Versailles settlement of 1919, when the German Question was tackled through diplomatic and financial pressure and military restrictions, but without directly intervening in the regeneration of the German political

[203] Luard, E., *Types of International Society*, pp. 305-8.

system. The Treaty of Versailles included occupation clauses. The Rhineland was occupied by France and Belgium from 1923-1936 as a result of Germany defaulting on her reparations obligations.[204] However, the Allied occupation of Germany in the aftermath of World War Two was undertaken with the determination to transform the nation.

The Allies employed a comprehensive approach to the treatment of the former Axis powers through the instrument of the Allied Commissions, consisting of representatives of the major Allied Powers. However, none of those institutions were as significant in the reconfiguration of the international order as the Allied Control Commission for Germany (ACC). The ACC was established on June 5, 1945 and supplemented by the agreement of September 20 of the same year.[205] The Instrument of Surrender issued by the major Allies on May 8, 1945 honoured the principle of unconditional surrender established by the Allies in Casablanca.[206] The Declaration on Germany of June 5, 1945, reiterated the principle of unconditional surrender. This meant that the main Allies, the United States, Britain, the Soviet Union and France (in the form of its Provisional Government) would assume

> supreme authority with respect to Germany, including all the powers possessed by the German Government, the High Command and any state, municipal, or local authority.

The Declaration contemplated the demilitarisation of Germany (articles 1-5, 7, 10, 13), denazification and Allied control of Germany (article 12).[207]

[204] Articles 428-432, Treaty of Versailles, June 28, 1919 http://history.acusd.edu/gen/text/versaillestreaty/vercontents.html.
[205] Cooperation by the ACC broke down as the Soviet representative withdrew on March 20, 1948. The ACC convened again in 1971, leading to agreement on transit arrangements in Berlin and during the unification talks in late 1989. The disbanding of the ACC was officially announced by the Two Plus Four Agreement of September 12, 1990, effective as of March 15, 1991.
[206] German Instrument of Surrender, May 8, 1945- http://en.wikisource.org/wiki/German_Instrument_of_Surrender_%288_May_1945%29.
[207] Declaration on Germany June 5, 1945- From *Documents on Germany under Occupation,* p. 29.

The Allies stipulated that authority in Germany would be exercised (on the instructions from their governments) by the British, American, Soviet and French Commanders-in-chief, each in his own zone of occupation, and also jointly, in matters affecting Germany as a whole. The ACC decisions were to be unanimous in order to ensure appropriate uniformity of action by the Commanders-in-Chief in their respective zones of occupation.[208] The ACC was supported by a Coordinating Committee and Control Staff. The Coordinating Committee was composed of Military, Naval, Air, Transport, Economic, Finance, Reparations, Deliveries and Restitutions, Internal Affairs and Communications, Legal, Prisoners of War and Displaced Persons and Manpower Directorates. There were four heads for each division, one for each occupying power. Its staff included military and civil personnel.

The Coordinating Committee carried out the Council's decisions, communicated them to the appropriate German bodies and supervised the day-to-day activities of the latter. United Nations organisations, if admitted by the Control Council to operate in Germany, were to be subordinate to the Allied control machinery and answerable to it.

Although this modus operandi would create the difficulties that brought about the bipolar outcome for Germany, the determination of the Allies to work together in matters pertaining to the reconstitution of the German political and social system is indicative of their willingness to apply intervention in the same manner as they employed it during the war. The ACC contributed to the transformation of Germany *because* the Allies were eager to apply the notions of intervention and coexistence.

Intervention extended to the control of the German economy. On September 20, 1945 Proclamation no. 2 of the ACC established that the Allies would

> exercise such control as they deem necessary over all or any part or aspect of German finance, agriculture, production and mining, public utilities, industry,

[208] Statement by the governments of the United Kingdom, the United States, the Soviet Union and the Provisional Government of the French Republic on Control Machinery, June 5, 1945- From *Documents on Germany under Occupation,* p. 36.

> trade...and over all related or ancillary matters, including the direction or prohibition of the manufacture, production, construction, treatment, use and disposal of any building, establishments, installations, public or private works, plant, equipment, products, materials, stock and resources.[209]

The Control Council agreed on a number of measures that would be pivotal for the political, legal and administrative organisation of post-war Germany. On November 6, 1945, through Directive no. 16, the Allies agreed to rearm the German police after the removal of personnel hostile to the occupation authorities.[210] The ACC also deliberated on the transfer of ethnic Germans from Austria, Czechosolovakia, Hungary and Poland into the four zones of occupation. On November 20, 1945 the ACC agreed that

> the entire German population from Poland (three and a half million persons) will be admitted to the Soviet and British zones of occupation in Germany...[and that] the entire German population from Czechoslovakia, Austria and Hungary (3,150,000 persons) will be admitted to the American, French, and the Soviet zones of occupation in Germany.[211]

This kind of intervention was particularly important because it reversed the historical trend of German expansion into Eastern Europe. Historically, the presence of *Volkdeutsche* in the East constituted a significant factor in the extension of the German borders well beyond the Oder-Neisse line. The transfer of ethnic Germans was probably undertaken in the belief that the measure would have confined the future German set up to a less extended geopolitical space. The significance of this undertaking still lingers on, as after

[209] Control Council Proclamation no. 2: Certain additional requirements imposed on Germany, September 20, 1945-From Von Oppen, B., Op. Cit., pp. 68-79.
[210] Control Council Directive no. 16: Arming of the German Police, November 6, 1945-From Von Oppen, B., Op. Cit., pp. 88-9.
[211] Control Council Plans for the transfer of the German population to be moved from Austria, Czechoslovakia, Hungary and Poland into the four occupied zones of Germany, November 20, 1945-From Von Oppen, B., Op. Cit., pp. 89-90.

reunification in 1989 Germany kept the same borders demarcated by the four occupation powers in 1945.

Further measures were carried out in order to prevent a militaristic resurgence of Germany. On May 13, 1946 Order no. 4 called for the confiscation of literature and material of a Nazi and militarist nature.[212] On August 20, 1946 Law no. 34 dissolved the German Armed Forces, including the

> Oberkommando der Wehrmacht (OKW), Oberkommando des Heeres (OKH), Reichsluftfahrtministerium (RLM), and Oberkommando der Kriegsmarine (OKM), all German land, naval and air forces, with all their organisations, staffs and institutions, including the general staff, the officers corps, reserve corps, military schools, war veteran organisations, and all other military and quasi-military organisations, together with all clubs and associations which serve to keep alive the military tradition in Germany.[213]

On October 12, 1946 Directive no. 40 established the policy to be followed by German politicians and the press. The Directive prohibited politicians and journalists from contributing 'towards the spreading of nationalistic, pan-Germanic, militarist, fascist or anti-democratic ideas' and from criticising Allied decisions made at CFM and ACC level.[214]

The elements described above point out to intervention within the context of commonly agreed rules and institutions, a legacy of the wartime practical association framework. Intervention geared to the transformation of Germany was implemented within the framework of coexistence. This model of direct intervention would be applied in other locales during the Cold War.[215] Both

[212] Control Council Order no. 4: Confiscation of literature and material of Nazi and militarist nature, May 13, 1946-From Von Oppen, B., Op. Cit., pp. 134-5.
[213] Control Council Law no. 34: Dissolution of the Wehrmacht, August 20, 1946-From Von Oppen, B., Op. Cit., pp. 151-2.
[214] Control Council Directive no. 38: the arrest and punishment of war criminals, Nazis and militarists and the internment, control and surveillance of potentially dangerous Germans, October 12, 1946- From Von Oppen, B., Op. Cit., pp. 168-79.
[215] The United States would be responsible for redesigning the political framework of post-war Japan through the promulgation of a new constitution. The 1947 Constitution included provisions that transformed Japanese society and the country's position in the international order;

Moscow and Washington would apply direct intervention in their spheres of influence in order to enforce adherence to the policy guidelines that sustained the superpowers' long range political and economic objectives. The United States would intervene in Latin America to enforce compliance with the system which sustained Washington's political and economic interests, as in Guatemala (1953), Brazil (1964) and Chile (1973). The Soviet Union would operate in a similar manner in Hungary (1956) and Czechoslovakia (1968). It would be precisely when direct intervention failed, as in the case of the events which unfolded in the aftermath of the Cuban Revolution, that the boundaries established by the spheres of influence system ran the risk of becoming blurred and prompted the risk of a systemic war. At the end of the Cold War, the concept of intervention would gain a new momentum. The Fukuyaman idea of the 'end of history', which echoes the Marxian notion of 'historical imperatives', was enshrined in the liberal credo of a 'new world order'. Intervention would also be influential in the reshaping of the post-Cold War international order according to the Washington Consensus and direct military and political involvement, as in the case of the Balkans and the Persian Gulf in the 1990s.

The intervention of the superpowers in the treatment of the German Question was crucial in the formation of a balance of power in Germany and Europe. The sphere of influence system which emerged after the war originated as the result of the pursuit of the national interest on the part of Moscow and Washington. This balance of power was primarily and decisively shaped in Germany before it became fait accompli in the rest of Europe.[216] During the war, the territorial division of Europe according to spheres of influence was discussed at length at inter-Allied level. During the early stages of the war, the Soviets did not want to press the Western Allies too hard on territorial issues. During the Anglo-Soviet Treaty discussions in London in May 1942, the Soviets agreed to a compromise proposal for the withdrawal from the Baltic

notably, article 9, which to this day states that the 'Japanese people renounce war as a sovereign right of the nation'.

[216] Interestingly, the concept of spheres of influence was mentioned in the Ribbentrop-Molotov Treaty of 1939.

region. In place of a secret agreement by which the British were to support Soviet claims to Romanian annexations, the Soviets asked only that Britain recognise the special interests of the Soviet Union in Romania and Finland. With Germany still ravaging the Soviet Union, the war effort took priority over territorial concerns and Stalin instructed Molotov to sign the Anglo-Soviet Treaty, which omitted all references to territorial boundaries.[217]

At the Teheran Conference, with the German Army already in retreat in the Eastern Front, Stalin reversed his position on the Baltic region. The Western powers tacitly acknowledged the legitimacy of Soviet territorial claims over Poland.[218] In October 1944 Churchill met Stalin in Moscow. Both leaders agreed that Bulgaria and Romania were to be areas largely under Soviet influence and that Greece would fall into the British sphere of influence. Britain and the Soviet Union were to equally share control in Yugoslavia and Hungary. In spite of Churchill's assurances to Hull that this was only applicable to war conditions, both statesmen understood that it represented a political division of the Balkans.[219] With both the Anglo-American military forces and the Red Army deep into Europe (from Normandy to Poland) the new political reality, enshrined in the 'Percentages Agreement' and confirmed at the Yalta Conference, laid down the prospect of a Soviet Eastern Europe and the possibility of US interventionism in Western Europe.

After the war, the Allies operated on the premise of a spheres of influence system. During 1945-6 the situation in Central and Eastern Europe was evolving toward sovietisation. However, Washington refrained from making any concerted efforts to prevent the imposition of Communist rule in Eastern Europe. The spheres of influence system in Germany (demarcated by the zones of occupation) became a 'peace of sorts' which informed inter-Allied relations in the international political system at large. The United States was prepared to

[217] Neumann, W., *Making The Peace*, p. 34.
[218] *Ibidem*, pp. 67-8.
[219] *Ibidem*, p. 76.

let Central and Eastern Europe become part of the Soviet sphere. At the same time, Washington focused its efforts on reconstituting Western Europe.[220]

Developments in Germany, where the Allies undertook an assiduous diplomatic and legal engagement, reassured all parties concerned of each other's aims and intentions in a tangible manner. The occupation of Germany created demarcation lines for the enforcement of the superpowers' national interest. A successful enforcement of those interests in Germany would provide the superpowers with the opportunity to expand and maintain their spheres of influence elsewhere in Europe.

The balance of power created during the 1943-8 period differed from previous attempts by great powers to organise the international political system. The spheres of influence system was sustained by two superpowers which had overwhelming capabilities to marshal the international political system without the need to engage in delicate multipolar alliances. Unlike the great powers of the Concert of Europe in the nineteenth century, the superpowers had the capacity to act unilaterally in their sphere of interests. Therefore, the emerging balance of power was more likely to fall apart because of internal rather than systemic causes.[221] The war in Europe created an opening for the permanent involvement of the United States in European affairs. In the space of 24 months after the end of the war, the United States succeeded in the task of politically emasculating Germany and in the creation of a non-autarkic Western European bloc. Western Germany, Western Europe, Britain and Japan became politically, economically and militarily integrated with the United States during the Cold War. This placed the United States in a position of advantage in relation to the Soviet Union. Both the United States and its Allies in the stronghold parts of the world benefited from this relationship. Conversely, the Soviet Union, forced to fight a war of national survival against Nazi Germany, was compelled to create a defensive sphere of influence almost exclusively in the

[220] See Lundestad, G., *The American Non-Policy Towards Eastern Europe 1943-1947.*
[221] See Waltz, K., *Theory of International Relations.*

heartland of Europe relying on the political and military coercion of the relatively poor countries of Central and Eastern Europe.

The failure of the Moscow CFM of 1947 in achieving economic unity for occupied Germany would be the catalyst in the consolidation of a Western policy, centered around the economic recovery of the Anglo-American zones. This policy would have a significant impact on the fate of Western Europe. Any success in the economic recovery of Bizonia was linked to the implementation of the ERP and the supply of German mineral resources to its neighbours. The Soviet Union, fearing encirclement by the West, construed the failure to achieve an agreement on German economic unity at the Moscow CFM as an opportunity to consolidate its own bloc.

The diplomatic breakdown at the Moscow CFM in 1947 enabled the Allies to pursue their long range objectives in Germany and Europe without constraints. Allied agreement at Moscow would have restored German unity. A united Germany would have enabled the possible emergence of a tripolar world, and the retreat of the United States and the Soviet Union into a less prominent position in the international political system. This would have signified a reversal of the 'grand design' envisaged by both superpowers. The Moscow CFM is another example of direct intervention by the superpowers in the making of the post-war international order. In this context, the policy of diplomatic breakdown *was* the policy of bloc-formation. By the time the Allies met at Moscow, the containment mindset prevailed in the US delegation. The Red Army was making sure that the area under its control adopted the political and economic policies dictated by Moscow. More importantly, Bizonia and the sovietisation of the Eastern zone ensured that the German Question could not be divorced from developments elsewhere in Europe. By accomplishing a diplomatic breakdown, the United States attained its goal of expanding the free market system of exchange through political and economic intervention. At the same time, a divided Germany reassured the Soviet Union that the former foe would not be able to exert any political influence in Central and Eastern Europe.

This balance of power system enjoyed a great deal of stability during the Cold War due to the bandwagoning of the former Western European powers into the Washington-led political and economic transnational structures.[222] The German Question also affected the role of the minor Western Allies, Britain and France. Faced with the loss of political and economic autonomy, the western parts of Germany and Europe had little choice but to bandwagon into the Atlantic system of collective security imposed by the United States.

In March 1946 a memorandum produced by Ernest Bevin, British Foreign Minister, summarised Britain's aims in Germany. There were five main points: first, security from a revival of German aggression; second, reasonable economic well-being in Germany and Europe; third, a reduction of the British occupation costs in Germany; fourth, the creation of a democratic and Western-minded Germany; and fifth, the restriction of Soviet influence as far to the east as possible.[223] Disagreements with France and the Soviet Union over Germany, a dire financial situation at home and the occupation costs in Germany (which the British paid for with the money from the $ 3.75 billion US loan) prompted Bevin, the Foreign Office and the Cabinet to press Washington for the formation of a US-led bloc, a US permanent presence in Europe and the rehabilitation of the Western zones of occupation in Germany.

[222] 'Bandwagoning' was coined by Quincy Wright in *A Study of War* (1942) and popularised by Kenneth Waltz in *Theory of International Politics* (1979). In the bandwagoning process, the political system of Washington's allies took second place to the economic priority attached to the 'grand design'. Spain was politically and economically isolated until 1955, when it became strategically important for the United States to foment a military presence on the Iberian peninsula, next to the Mediterranean Sea and the Strait of Gibraltar. Salazar's Portugal was the only non-democracy amongst the founding members of NATO in 1949, which reflected Portugal's role as an ally against communism during the Cold War. After liberation from Nazi Germany, Greece experienced an equally bitter civil war, caused by the differences that emerged between left-wing and right-wing resistance forces. Civil war began between the Democratic Army of Greece and right-wing forces which had the support of the Hellenic Army. During the 1950s and 1960s, Greece experienced a gradual and significant economic growth, aided by grants and loans by the United States through the Marshall Plan. After participating with United Nations forces in the Korean conflict, Turkey, another non-democracy, joined the NATO in 1952, becoming a bulwark against Soviet expansion into the Mediterranean.

[223] PRO: CAB 129/9, CP (46) 156, Gen 121/1, 'The Future of Germany and the Ruhr', Ernest Bevin, 11 March 1946.

French policy over Germany also contributed to the process of bandwagoning. France influenced the bloc-formation process by preventing the setting of central administrative bodies in Germany, therefore giving the other Allies leeway to pursue the organisation of Bizonia and the sovietisation of the Eastern zone. French policy on Germany during the 1944-7 period rotated around Paris' desire for a guarantee against future German aggression. French policy was underpinned by political as well as economic considerations. Paris wanted to avoid a resurgence of the German nationalism which had prompted three invasions of its territory since 1870. France demanded that the Ruhr be severed politically and economically from the rest of Germany and placed under the control of those states that could make use of its coal, going as far as using its power of veto in the ACC and the CFM to reject any proposal for German unification.[224] Paris' stringent policy on Germany began to shift in 1947, when the Soviet threat began to assume a more peremptory character and the German problem changed in nature and urgency.[225] By 1947 the French demand on access to German coal was met by the Western Allies, prompting the creation of the trizonal arrangement and the co-opting of France into the Washington-led bloc. The French bandwagoning signaled the end of the rivalry which haunted the international order since the late nineteenth century. With France unable to muster the political leverage to influence the international political system and Germany having surrendered its state to the Allies, the way was paved for a new order of things in Europe.

Although the process of bandwagoning meant a partial constraint on independent manoeuvering by London and Paris, the input of the minor occupation powers in the treatment of the German Question is indicative of the significance of intervention as one of the primary institutions of the Cold war international order. French policy on Germany would be crucial for the accomplishment of European integration and the Europeanisation of the German Question, as epitomised in the creation of the Common Market in 1957 and the

[224] Smyser, W.R., *From Yalta to Berlin: the Cold War Struggle over Germany*, p. 48.
[225] Schuman, R., *French Policy Towards Germany Since the War*, Lecture delivered on October 29, 1953 at the Royal Institute of International Affairs (Oxford University Press), p. 7.

Franco-German Treaty in 1959. The legacy of the French influence in the shaping of the role of Germany in the post-war international order would become evident at the end of the Cold War, when the French President François Mitterrand pressed for further economic integration and the creation of a common European currency as part of the German reunification process.

The 1943-1990 system had a significant effect in the consolidation of political and economic integration in Europe. Western Europe would become more politically and economically integrated than ever before in history. This integration process (sponsored and assisted by Washington) would abolish the balance of power system within Western Europe which operated regularly since 1648. The 1943-8 period profoundly altered intra-European relations. The foreseeable demise of the British Empire led to the idea of closer economic links between Britain and Europe. The United States, fearful of the onset of another economic depression, was interested in creating the conditions for a liberal system of exchange. This provided Washington with the impetus to give political and economic sponsorship to the process of Western European integration. Fears of another encirclement by the West compelled Moscow to carve a sphere of influence in Eastern Europe and marshal a simultaneous integration process with her satellites.

With Germany deprived of any say in the realignment of the post-war international system, the integration process in Western Europe would assume the characteristics desired by Washington. A similar process would unfold beyond the Iron Curtain, with Moscow dictating the modality of Eastern European integration. The experience of the war and the possibility of military conflict between the two Europes gave meaning to the process of integration. The experience of the United States, with the tenfold expansion of state intervention in the economy since the Great Depression[226] was mirrored in Western Europe, where the Welfare States were introduced and major industries nationalised. The incentive for integration in Western Europe

[226] See DiLorenzo, T.J., *How Capitalism Saved America-The Untold History of our Country. From the Pilgrims to the Present.*

stemmed from the political sponsorship provided by the Marshall Plan and the relative decline of France and Britain vis-à-vis the superpowers. France, Germany, Italy and the Low Countries had complex industrial networks and a geo-economic potential which facilitated their absorption into a common economic space. Integration was facilitated by the subordination of Germany to supranational institutions, the creation of an Atlantic linkage (which placed the ultimate responsibility for the security of Western Europe in the hands of Washington) and the threat posed by the Soviet Union. This transformation proved to have a lasting effect. The political and economic integration of Western Europe in the aftermath of World War Two revolved around the premises that would inform the process of absorption of East Germany and the former Soviet bloc after 1989-90. The outcome of the German Question produced a situation in which preying upon regional neighbours had become irrational. Western European civil societies would be empowered to constrain state-action. Sub-national and supranational institutions and networks became an important element in this process. The depoliticisation of Western European nationalisms, the creation of a supranational European community and, to an extent never seen before, the setting of regional interdependence as the prime source of Western European wealth, aided the process of integration.[227]

The political and economic integration of Western Europe unfolded as the immediate result of the treatment of the German Question. The outcome of the German Question transcended the conflictual aspects of the Cold War, as it established a successful framework for inter-state cooperation through the transformation of Germany's position in Europe and the role of the former imperial powers in the post-war international order.

The doctrine of 'correlation of forces' informed Moscow's intervention in the formation of the balance of power. For the Soviet Union, intervention became a Rationalist tool for the attainment of vital interests. Intervention was applied in the sovietisation of Eastern Europe, by forcing the countries beyond

[227] Puchala, D., *Western Europe* in Jackson, R.H. and James, A., *States in a Changing World- A Contemporary Analysis*, pp. 76-7.

the Iron Countries to reject ERP aid, and in the isolation of Tito's Yugoslavia. The concept of 'correlation of forces' (*sootnoshenie sil*) conveys the idea of a relationship or distribution of power.[228] In practical terms it entailed that if the calculation was favourable, then the appropriate tactical action would be that of advancing the Soviet cause without generating undue strategic risk.[229] The doctrine of 'correlation of forces' played a significant part in the development of post-war Soviet strategic thought. World War Two had forced the Soviet Union to reassess her long-term strategic weaknesses. This reassessment forced the Soviet leadership to carve a sphere of influence in Germany and Europe, catapulting the country into superpower status and ensuring the accomplishment of its security goals. The Soviets worked on two different strategies simultaneously. On one hand they proclaimed the unity of Germany at the ACC and during the CFM negotiations. At the same time, they prompted the emergence of a bipolar situation in Germany by sovietising their zone of occupation, and impeding the rehabilitation of Germany as a single unit by insisting on the extraction of reparations from the Western zones. This responded to long-dated (and rather justified) fears of an anti-Soviet bloc which would include Germany.

The intervention of the superpowers in the treatment of the German Question secured the creation of a bipolar international order. The only entity strategically capable of becoming a 'third force' in the post-war international order (balancing against the Soviet Union and the United States) would have been an independent and neutral Germany. The idea of a 'third force' was toyed with in Britain and France. However, the political and economic dislocation caused by the war and the looming conflict between the superpowers rendered impossible the emergence of a neutral Germany and an independent Europe.

[228] Garthoff, R., 'The Concept of the Balance of Power in Soviet Policy Making', *World Politics*, p. 88.
[229] Garthoff, R., *Soviet Military Doctrine*, p. 91. For the concept of 'correlation of forces' see Hansen, J., *Correlation of Forces: Four Decades of Soviet Military Development*. Also, Lider, J., *Correlation of forces: an analysis of Marxist-Leninist concepts*.

Germany managed to integrate the economic resources of Western Europe during the Nazi period. The Nazi leaders also worked towards establishing the foundations of an autarkic and self-sufficient socio-economic system in Europe. The reconstitution of Germany as a unified autonomous unit would have entailed the withdrawal of the United States from Western European after the war and the possible absorption of the Central and Eastern European economies on the part of the Germans. The idea of an independent Germany was pervasive in the Soviet leadership during the 1943-8 period. Furthermore, an independent Germany would have found a rapprochement with the Soviet Union easier and more productive, as Moscow would have probably placed fewer constraints on German sovereignty, provided her security requirements were met. The Stalin Note of 1952 and Lavrentii Beria's suggestion for the reunification of Germany in 1953 are eloquent examples of the ambivalent position of the Soviet Union on the German Question.[230] For the superpowers, intervention in Germany became the medium by which they enforced their national interests in the wider spectrum of the post-war international order. By doing so, intervention, the instrument that facilitated the successful culmination of the war, became one of the primary institutions of the Cold War international order.

[230] Soviet terms for reunification included the reestablishment of Germany as a united state within the boundaries established by the provisions of the Potsdam Conference, a single united German government to play a role in the negotiations of the peace treaty and the withdrawal of all occupation forces within one year. Following the date on which a treaty would come into effect, political parties and organisations were to have 'free' activity. Germany was to have its own national armed forces and would be allowed to manufacture munitions for these forces. Germany would also be given access to world markets and former members of the German armed forces and of the Nazi Party, except for convicted war criminals, could join in establishing a peaceful and democratic Germany. For an account of the Stalin Note see Steninger, R. *The German Question: The Stalin Note of 1952 and the Problem of Reunification.* Also, see Walko, John W.. *The Balance of Empires: United States' Rejection of German Reunification and Stalin's March Note of 1952.*

IX The Role of Coexistence in the Post-war International Order

Coexistence would become the second most prominent institution of the Cold War international order. This development was brought about by the formation of a spheres of influence system, shaped through the intervention of the superpowers. The practical association formed for the purposes of the prosecution of the war against Germany, left the main Allies with the responsibility of creating an international order diametrically opposed to the ideology of the Axis and one in which Communism and Western democracy would be able to coexist.

The duration and nature of the wartime practical association, as well as the responsibility of realigning the international political system after the war, created a situation of coexistence between the superpowers. In spite of the gradual and irreversible breakdown of the practical association framework after the war there was no 'cognitive closure' between the Allies[231] as they were fully aware of each other's intentions and needs. The possibility of conflict was restrained by the same instruments on which the practical association framework rested during the war: international law, diplomacy and the acceptance of the spheres of influence system. Ideological diversity required the operation of a legal framework that would enable the establishment of a post-war international order based on coexistence. The nascent post-war

[231] See Lebow, R.N., *Between Peace and War-The Nature of International Crisis.*

society of states acknowledged the need to cooperate and marshal the international order.

The ACC was the main diplomatic forum in the discussion of the issues regarding the German Question and reflected not just the divergence of interests, but also the legal and ethical dimension of the responsibilities that burdened the superpowers. The spirit of cooperation and the willingness on the part of the Allies to achieve transformation in Germany would extend to the management of the international political system. Achieving a 'peace of sorts' in regards to the most crucial element in the realignment of the post-war international order would serve to create strict demarcation lines in Europe and therefore maintain a non-disruptive international order during the Cold War.

Through the medium of the ACC, the Allies were able to debate the issues regarding the German Question on a continual basis. Notwithstanding the conflict of interests that arose out of political developments in the zones of occupation and the international political system at large, during the early period of the occupation (1945-6), the ACC accomplished the task of laying down the foundations for the social and political reorganisation of Germany by eliminating all the vestiges of the Nazi political system. As Germany underwent a process of full-blown polarisation during the 1947-8 period, the ACC passed into law a considerable number of measures which ensured the transformation of Germany. This was indicative of the spirit of cooperation between the superpowers. Measures included the repeal of Nazi legislation concerning hereditary farms, the termination of German insurance operations abroad, exchange of parcels between Berlin and the zones of occupation, a law to combat venereal disease, the liquidation of the Krupp steelworks, the abrogation of certain provisions in the German penal law, and a law providing for interzonal exchange of printed material.[232]

The ACC became the medium which facilitated an orderly passage into a bipolar arrangement for Germany before it became fully operational in Europe.

[232] Clay, L., *Decision in Germany*, pp. 155-6.

The superpowers' diplomatic engagement in the management of the occupation contributed to generate a spirit of coexistence that would inform the Cold War international order. Because the Allies did not discuss the issue of a peace treaty with Germany until the Moscow CFM in 1947, the ACC took on the main diplomatic role on the German Question. The diplomatic and legal framework of the ACC had liberal aspects that would inform the shape of things to come not just in Germany but in the international order at large. It is partly due to the work done by the Allies at the ACC that a convivial spheres of influence system unfolded in Europe. The ACC represented the nucleus of an international society for it constituted the main medium of inter-Allied diplomacy, negotiations and law-making in regards to Germany. It solidified the Rationalist legacy of the wartime period as the Allies continued to engage in the legal and diplomatic process in spite of their ideological diversity. This pattern would continue to inform the order of things in Germany and Europe, inasmuch as it would put restraints on unilateral action by the superpowers. The legal structure guiding the occupation of Germany was informed by the practical association framework established during the war. The ACC would have a transformative effect in the international order for it reduced Germany to a subordinate position in the international political system and propelled a continuous show of strength between two emerging camps in a magnitude not seen elsewhere in the international political system. The Red Army established a position of dominance in the Eastern Europe countries and served as a catalyst for their gradual transition into a Soviet-led bloc. Conversely, in Germany the Allies were forced, to an extent unseen elsewhere, to engage in permanent diplomacy and negotiation, because of the significance of the outcome of the German Question in the configuration of the post-war international order.

The Allied Control Council and its Coordinating Committee provided the inter-Allied occupation structure with a forum to discuss and shape policy. The ACC served as the main forum of inter-Allied occupation policy and gave a Rationalist framework to the treatment of the German Question, not only through the making of inter-Allied policy but also by creating a common cause façade which would enable the practical association to unravel within the principle of ethical cohabitation. The nature and extent of the occupation structure put in place by the Allies in Germany had no precedent in modern history. It denoted the Allies' willingness to work together in order to achieve a workable settlement in Germany. The complexity of the occupation structure is indicative of the importance of the German Question in the configuration of the post-war international order. The Tripartite Commissions in the liberated countries operated without the convivialism of the ACC. Unlike Germany, no other former Axis power could tip the balance of power towards any of the superpowers. The Allies agreed on the measures that would become influential in securing a permanent inter-Allied dialogue and presence in Germany.

Coexistence manifested itself in the creation of a bipolar solution for Germany and Europe. The failure of the Moscow and London CFMs served as catalysts for the consolidation of bipolar diplomacy over Germany and bloc-formation instead of a motive for all-out confrontation. The division of Germany became a distinct possibility from the moment the war ended. Remarkably though, after the implementation of Bizonia and the gradual sovietisation of the Eastern Zone, the road to partition was paved without disruptive conflict. The unfolding of the Berlin Blockade shows how much the Western powers and the Soviet Union valued the convenience of a Rationalist unraveling of four power control in Germany. The probing by both sides was highly calculated and both preferred the embarrassment of making concessions instead of risking a full-blown conflagration. On June 25, 1948 Clay gave the order to launch a massive airlift (ultimately lasting 462 days) that flew supplies into the Western-held sectors of Berlin during 1948-1949. By the time the blockade ended on May 11, 1948, 278,228 flights were made and 2,326,406 tons of food and supplies were delivered to Berlin. Tipton points to the 'legalistic distinctions' made by both the Soviet Union and the United States in order to prevent the situation from escalating into an all-out war. The United States refused to acquiesce to Clay's request for an American military breach into Berlin. At the same time, the Soviet Union did not challenge the passage of aircraft to feed the Western sector of the city or the transfer of Berlin's legislature into the Western sector.[233] According to Shlaim, the Soviets had minimum and maximum goals in imposing the blockade; the maximum aim was to halt the formation of a West German government while the minimum aim was to carry the division of Germany to its logical conclusion by liquidating the Western enclave in Berlin. Shlaim also argues that Soviet behaviour during the crisis was very cautious as at no point did Moscow intend to replace political pressure with military action.[234] The Berlin Blockade, the hottest confrontation of the Allies over Germany thus far, is an example of political brinkmanship which allows us to conclude that while the superpowers were willing to enforce their national interest with regard to the German Question, they were extremely cautious in avoiding a systemic conflict.

The process of polarisation occurred within the context of continued diplomatic engagement. The bipolar outcome reached in Germany did not stop the process of diplomatic engagement on the issues pertaining to the international political system at large. This differed significantly from the attitude taken by the Allies at Casablanca regarding the Nazi regime. When the conflict intensified, as during the Berlin Blockade, none of the superpowers called for 'unconditional surrender'. This implied a principle of recognition and convivialism which provided legitimacy to the nascent international political system. Soviet ambitions of a foothold in Germany and Eastern Europe did not completely contradict the American objective of a liberal economic order and the creation of a sphere of influence responsive to the pursuit of its national interest. The creation of Bizonia and the Western bloc was not designed to prevent the Soviet Union from establishing an East German state or securing a foothold in Eastern Europe but rather to solidify the continuation of the policies that created the wartime expansion of the American economy.

[233] Tipton, F. B., *A History of Modern Germany Since 1815*, p. 505.

[234] Shlaim A., *The partition of Germany and the origins of the Cold War*, p.134-5. For an account of the Berlin Blockade see Miller R. G., *To save a city: the Berlin airlift, 1948-1949*; Shlaim, A., *The United States and the Berlin Blockade, 1948-1949: a study in crisis decision-making*; Gottlieb., M., *The German peace settlement and the Berlin crisis*; and Davison, W. P., *The Berlin blockade: a study in Cold War politics*.

Superpower interaction concocted a stalemate in the epicenter and shifted the flash points to the periphery. As the possibility of disruptive conflict was seen as 'irrational', the Cold War would be mostly fought with a symbolic perspective in mind and restrained by the same instruments on which the practical association framework was laid down in 1943-5: law, diplomacy and the acceptance of the balance of power system.

Ⅹ The Origins of the Cold War in Perspective

The divergence of interests between the superpowers ultimately brought about the bipolar outcome in Germany and Europe. However, conflict overlapped with the entrenchment of a diplomatic and legal framework capable of sustaining a non-disruptive international order in which the superpowers would be able to pursue their national interest within clearly defined spheres of influence. Significantly, these developments facilitated the unfolding of a transformation in the society of states. Dealing with the German Question entailed the undertaking of a significant transformation of the country and subsequently, of the society of states as a whole. The denazification process that unfolded in Germany through the inter-Allied occupation had a revolutionist effect in the defeated nation and created several transformations in the states system.

During the 1943-8 period, ideological rivalries, which loomed primarily as the result of dealing with Germany on and off the battlefield, were reflected in the configuration of post-war international society. In effect, *the concern with ideology* became the ideology of the post-war international society.[235] Furthermore, the disruptive nature of the Hitlerite quest for domination in Europe would create an extension and an institutionalisation of international society unparalleled in the history of the international political system. Pointing

[235] Luard, E., *Types of international Society*, p. 69.

to an internationalisation of the system, Luard maintains that ideological loyalties (which transcend national boundaries) become as important in determining action as national loyalties, as states are more affected by developments elsewhere.[236] As the states-system expanded outside its European core, the extent over which a general balance of power was to be maintained, increased correspondingly.[237]

The treatment of the German Question from the Casablanca Conference of 1943 until the breakdown of four power control in 1948 was the most significant factor in the creation and evolution[238] of the post-war international order. The literature available on the German Question has so far attempted to explain isolated aspects of the subject. By using a more comprehensive approach, this study has shown that in the interaction of the superpowers in the treatment of the German Question, elements of conflict, legality and cooperation overlapped and shaped the position of Germany in the post-war international order. This work also contributed to determine the extent of the influence of the treatment of the German Question on the origins of the Cold War and the making post-war international order. Like the treatment of the German Question, the realignment of the post-war international order unfolded within the boundaries imposed by two superpowers labouring under highly calculated political moves, which although responding to the national interest, were restrained in their scope of action. The Allies set the path for the reconciliation of Germany's legitimate claims in the international political system and the elimination of the possibility of a post-war German challenge to the international order. *The German Question was the most important issue in the reordering of world politics because of the extent to which all other situational factors were linked to its outcome.* There would have been no successful outcome for the superpowers elsewhere in Europe (as far as their

[236] *Ibidem*, pp. 103-4.
[237] Wight, M., 'The Balance of Power and International Order' in James, A. (ed), *The Bases of International Order-Essays in Honour of C A W Manning*, pp. 100-8.
[238] For the evolution of the Cold War in Germany see Mitchell, O., *The Cold War in Germany-Overview, Origins and Intelligence Wars* and Burchett, W., *Cold War in Germany*.

'grand design' interests were concerned) without a viable solution in Germany. The treatment of the German Question created a modus operandi for superpower interaction which would be successfully transferred to the management of the Cold War international order.

The treatment of the German Question determined to a significant extent the roadmap to the post-war international order and helped to shape the diplomacy and institutions that would inform superpower interaction during the Cold War. The treatment of the German Question provided the superpowers with the opportunity to delineate their national interest priorities in the post-war scenario. Dealing with the German Question would also become the signposting exercise during the Cold War. The centrality of Germany as the originating factor of the Cold War meant that not only the scope of conflict, but also the working of diplomatic and legal arrangements and the possibility of transformation in the international political system would be negotiated through the management of the German Question. The Cold War international order would end in the same way it began: through the orderly resolution of the German Question. The reunification of Germany and the European continent in 1989-90 would have similar characteristics to the process of partition: conflict and cooperation cohabited, framed within a well-established legal and diplomatic system. It is within that context that the superpowers created and unraveled the Cold War.

Acknowledgements

I wish to thank Professor John W Young and the members of staff at the School of History of Nottingham University, especially Dr Richard Gaunt, Dr Andrew Cobbing, Dr Nick Thomas, Dr Chris Goto-Jones and Dr Sheryllynne Haggerty, who entrusted me with the wonderful task of teaching history seminars at the School of History of Nottingham University. Dr Nigel Aston opened the doors of the School of Historical Studies at Leicester University for me. During my time as a MA tutor at Leicester, many an afternoon were spent charting the German Question. Those afternoons contributed in a significant manner to the outcome of this project. Dr Karl Wilds of the German Department at Nottingham University gave me the chance to teach seminars on the Brandt chancellorship and I am grateful for being given such an opportunity. My thanks go Dr Peter Cunich at Hong Kong University, Dr Brad Williams at the National University of Singapore, Professor Helen Meller of Nottingham University and Professor Barry Buzan of the London School of Economics for giving me the chance to present papers on various aspects of the German Question.

My acknowledgment and thanks also go to the staff at the British Library, the Library of Congress in Washington DC and the libraries of the London School of Economics and Political Science, Birkbeck College, University

College London and the University of Nottingham. I acknowledge Crown Copyright for materials consulted at the National Archives (Kew Gardens, London). I also acknowledge the National Archives (Washington DC), for letting me comb their State, SWNCC and Treasury files. I am thankful for the assistance provided by their staff, particularly Matt Olson at College Park, MD.

I would like to extend particular thanks to my lecturers and teachers at Birkbeck College (University of London), my alma mater, which provided me, *in nocte consilium*, with the best training anyone could hope for in the fields of history, philosophy and politics, particularly Dr. Geoffrey Thomas, Dr. Bill Tompson, Dr. Mark Cain and Dr. Jan Hancock.

My immense gratitude goes to Monique Paté, a great New Yorker, for getting things done.

I thank Pietro Condemi, who supported this project and believed in it.

An undertaking such as this could not have been carried out without the support and love of my wonderful parents. I thank them for everything they gave me since I was a kid: love, laughter and a thirst for knowledge.

Finally, I dedicate this work to the most fragrant and exquisite rose of Yorkshire: my wife Sarah, whose love and generosity knows no boundaries.

Bibliography

Primary Sources

Archival sources

National Archives, Kew Gardens, London:

- FO 371, 945
- CAB 130, 129

National Archives, College Park, Maryland:

- US Treasury, 'Suggested Post-Surrender Program', September 1, 1944, RG 107, ASW 370.8, Germany, MMNA
- State Files 59
- General Records of the Department of the Treasury-Records of the Assistant Secretary of the Treasury. Re: monetary and international affairs Chronological file of H D White- Nov 1934-Apr 1946
- Miscellaneous German Files 1943-54 E1174.E
- SWNCC Files 15, 269, 257, 327, 303, 309, 283
- Interdepartmental and Intradepartmental Committee SWNCC- Decimal File 1944-49 Box 65

Official Publications

Bull Papers, Bodleian Library, Oxford

Department of State Bulletin, November 8, 1941 (Washington, DC: Government Printing Office) (1941)

Documents Diplomatiques Français 1945, Tome II (1er Julliet-31 Decembre), (Ministère des Affaires Étrangeres, Commission de Publications des Documents Diplomatiques Français, Imprimerie Nationale, Paris) (2000)

Documents Diplomatiques Français 1946, Tome I (1er Janvier-30 Juin), (Ministère des Affaires Étrangeres, Commission de Publications des Documents Diplomatiques Français , Imprimerie Nationale, Paris) (2000)

Documents on British Policy Overseas (London: HMSO) (Series I, Vol I) (1991)-Eastern Europe, August 1945-April 1946

Foreign Relations of the United States *(FRUS)* 1942, vol. III, Europe, United States Government Printing Office, Washington, DC, 1969

FRUS 1942, The Conference at Washington 1941-2 and Casablanca 1943 United States Government Printing Office, Washington, DC, 1969

FRUS 1943, Conferences at Cairo and Teheran 1943 United States Government Printing Office, Washington, DC, 1969

FRUS Conference at Quebec 1944 United States Government Printing Office, Washington, DC, 1969

FRUS, 1945, Vol. III, European Advisory commission; Austria; Germany, United States Government Printing Office, Washington, DC, 1969

FRUS 1945 Conferences at Malta and Yalta United States Government Printing Office, Washington, DC, 1969

FRUS, 1946, Vol. V, The British Commonwealth; Western and Central Europe, United States Government Printing Office, Washington, DC, 1969

Harley M. Kilgore Papers, West Virginia and Regional History Collection, West Virginia University, Morgantown

Schuman, R., *French Policy Towards Germany Since the War*, Lecture delivered on 29.10.1953 at the Royal Institute of International Affairs (Oxford University Press)

'Stenograph of a Public lecture', April 24, 1947 by Prof. Isakhov Moiseevich Faingar 'Germany and Reparations'

Von Oppen, Beate Ruhm, (ed) *Documents of Germany under Occupation 1945-1954*. Issued under the auspices of the Royal Institute of International Affairs (London, New York, Toronto: OUP) (1955)

War-Peace Study, Reparations Policy Toward Germany, March 18, 1943, Economic and Financial Group (CFR)

Woodward, E. L., *British foreign policy in the Second World War/ Vol.5,* (London: H.M.S.O.) (1976)

Memoirs

Acheson, D., *Present at the Creation: My Years in the State Department* (NY: Norton) (1969)

Bryant, A., *The Turn of the Tide* (Garden City, N.Y.: Doubleday and Company) (1957)

Churchill, W., *The Second World War*, Six Volumes (London: The Reprint Society) (1955)

Clay, L., *Decision in Germany* (Melbourne, London, Toronto: William Heinemann Ltd.) (1950)

Kennan, G., *Memoirs, 1925-50* (New York: Atlantic, Little, Brown) (1967)

Murphy, R., *Diplomat Among Warriors* (London: Collins) (1964)

Speer, A., *Inside the Third Reich*, (New York: Avid Books) (1970)

Strang, W., *Home and Abroad*, (London: Andre Deutsch) (1956)

Ulbricht, W., *Whither Germany? Speeches and Essays on the National Question*, (Dresden: Zeit Im Bild Publishing House) (1966)

Electronic Sources

Anglo-American Mutual Aid Agreement: http://www.ibiblio.org/pha/policy/1942/420223b.html

Andrei Zhdanov speech September 22, 1947:
www.uncg.edu/~jwjones/world/readings/zhdanovspeech.html
Article 42-UN Charter http://www.un.org/aboutun/charter
Articles 428-432, Treaty of Versailles, June 28, 1919:
http://history.acusd.edu/gen/text/versaillestreaty/vercontents.html
British Foreign Office files:
http://www.fco.gov.uk/servlet/Front?pagename=OpenMarket/Xcelerate/ShowPage&c=Page&cid=1007029395375
Casablanca Declaration, February 12, 1943:
http://www.yale.edu/lawweb/avalon/wwii/casablan.htm
Charter of Paris for a New Europe, Paris 19-21, 1990:
www1.umn.edu/humanrts/peace/docs/charterparis.html
Conference on Security and Co-operation in Europe, Final Act, Helsinki, August 1, 1975: www.hri.org/docs/Helsinki75.html
Convention on the Prevention and Punishment of the Crime of Genocide, 9 December 1948:
http://www.icrc.org/ihl.nsf/52d68d14de6160e0c12563da005fdb1b/a2ec826e5d083098c125641e0040690d?OpenDocument
Declaration by the United Nations, January 1, 1942:
civicwebs.com/cwvlib/.../un/e_united_nations_declaration_1942.htm
Directive to Commander-in-Chief of United States Forces of Occupation Regarding the Military Government of Germany; April 1945 (JCS 1067): usa.usembassy.de/etexts/ga3-450426.pdf
English School website: source of notes on the British International www.leeds.ac.uk/polis/englishschool
Extracts from Marshall Speech at Harvard University June 5, 1947:
http://www.oecd.org/document/10/0,2340,en_2649_201185_1876938_1_1_1_1,00.html
FDR Annual Message to Congress January 6, 1942,
http://www.ibiblio.org/pha/policy/1942/420106a.html

German Instrument of Surrender, May 8, 1945: http://en.wikisource.org/wiki/German_Instrument_of_Surrender_%288_May_1945%29

Kennan, G., Telegram to the Secretary of State, February 22, 1946-http://www.gwu.edu/~nsarchiv/coldwar/documents/episode-1/kennan.htm

Lend Lease Act March 11, 1941: http://www.history.navy.mil/faqs/faq59-23.htm

Nazi Party documents-www.hitler.org

Nikolai, N., Soviet Ambassador in Washington, Telegram, September 1946: http://www.mtholoyoke.edu/acad/intrel/novikov.htm

Novikov, N., Telegram to Moscow, September 1946: http://www.mtholyoke.edu/acad/intrel/novikov.htm

Preliminary Agreement Between the United States and the United Kingdom, February 23, 1942: http://www.yale.edu/lawweb/avalon/decade/decade04.htm

Protocol of the Proceedings-Potsdam Conference, August 1, 1945: http://www.yale.edu/lawweb/avalon/decade/decade17.htm

Roosevelt Presidential Library files: http://www.fdrlibrary.marist.edu/

Speech delivered by US President Woodrow Wilson to a joint session of the United States Congress on January 8, 1918: http://usinfo.state.gov/usa/infousa/facts/democrac/51.htm

The National Security Archive files: http://www.gwu.edu/~nsarchiv/

The Truman Presidential Library files: http://www.trumanlibrary.org/

The Atlantic Charter, August 14, 1941: http://usinfo.state.gov/usa/infousa/facts/democrac/53.htm

Treaty on the Final Settlement with Respect to Germany, Moscow, September 12, 1990: http://usa.usembassy.de/etexts/2plusfour8994e.htm

Truman Presidential Library files: http://www.trumanlibrary.org

Yalta Declaration, February 11, 1945: http://www.yale.edu/lawweb/avalon/wwii/yalta.htm

Secondary Sources

Alexander, B., *How Hitler Could Have Won World War II-The Fatal Errors that Led to Nazi Defeat* (Three Rivers Press: New York) (2000)

Alexander, Y., and Pluchinsky, D. A., *Europe's Red Terrorists: The Fighting Communist Organizations* (London: Routledge) (1992)

Allen, R.G.D., 'Mutual Aid between the US and the British Empire, 1941-5', *Journal of the Royal Statistical Society*, No.109 :3, 1946

Almeida, J. M. de, 'Challenging Realism by Returning to History: the British Committee's Contribution to IR 40 Years On', *International Relations*, 17(3), 2003

Alperovitz, G.:

- *Atomic Diplomacy: Hiroshima and Potsdam* (London: Pluto) (1994)
- *The Decision to Use the Atomic Bomb* (New York: Vintage) (1995)

Ambrose S., and Brinkley D., *Rise to Globalism: American Foreign Policy since 1938* (New York and London: Penguin) (1997)

Anderson K, and Hurrell A., *Hedley Bull on International Society* (Basingstoke: Macmillan) (1999)

Anderson, M. S., *The Rise of Modern Diplomacy 1450-1919* (London: Longman and Hamilton) (1993)

Annan, N., *Changing Enemies: The Defeat and Regenerations of Germany,* (Harper Collins Publishers: London) (1995)

Armstrong, A., *Unconditional Surrender: The Impact of the Casablanca Policy upon World War II* (New Brunswick: Rutgers University Press) (1961)

Arkes, H., *Bureaucracy, the Marshall Plan, and the National Interest* (Princeton and New Jersey: Princeton University Press) (1972)

Aubert, L. (Ed), *Contrôle de l'Allemagne: Control of Germany*, [prepared by the Royal Institute of International Affairs and other bodies for a Conference held in Holland, October, 1947, and April, 1948] (Paris: Rivière) (1949)

Ayçoberry, P, *The Nazi Question: an Essay on the Interpretations of National Socialism 1922-1975* (London and Henley: Routledge and Kegan Paul) (1989)

Backer, J. H., *The Decision to Divide Germany: American Foreign Policy in Transition* (Duke University Press: Durham, NC) (1978)

Baigent, M. and Leigh, R., *Secret Germany-Stauffenberg and the Mystical Crusade against Hitler* (Arrow Books: Random House) (2006)

Bailey, T., *America Faces Russia* (Oxford: Oxford University Press) (1950)

Balfour, M.:

- *Germany: The Tides of Power* (London and New York: Routledge) (1992)
- 'Another Look at Unconditional Surrender', *International Affairs*, Vol 46, no. 4, October 1970

Bandow, Doug (Ed.): *U.S. Aid to the Developing World: A Free Market Agenda* (Washington: Heritage Found) (1985)

Bassett, R., *Hitler's Chief Spy: The Wilhelm Canaris Mystery* (London: Cassell) (2005)

Baylis J. and Smith S. (Ed.), *The Globalization of World Politics: An Introduction to International Relations* (Oxford: Oxford University Press) (2001)

Beaumont, R., 'The Bomber Offensive as a Second Front', *Journal of Contemporary History*, 22, January 1987

Beevor, A., *Berlin-The Downfall 1945* (London: Penguin Books) (2004)

Behncke, M., *Democratization or Sovietization? The Development of the Soviet Zone of Occupation in Germany 1945-1950 in the Light of Recent Findings* (PhD thesis, Pacific Western University, 1983)

Bellamy, A., (ed), *International Society and its Critics* (Oxford: Oxford University Press) (2005)

Bercuson, D. and Herwig H., *One Christmas at Washington: Churchill and Roosevelt Forge the Grand Alliance* (London: Phoenix Paperbacks) (2006)

Berghahn, V R.:
- *Modern Germany: Society, Economy and Politics in the Twentieth Century* (Cambridge: Cambridge University Press) (1987)
- *The Americanisation of West German Industry, 1945-1973* (Berg and New York: Leamington Spa) (1986)
- 'The Allies and the Reorientation of German Culture after 1945', *Diplomatic History*, Volume 30, Number 3, June 2006, pp. 545-548(4)

Berridge, G., *Diplomacy-Theory and Practice* (London: Prentice Hall) (1995)

Bird, K., *The Chairman: John J. McCloy-The Making of the American Establishment* (New York: Simon & Schuster) (1992)

Bernstein, B., (ed.) *Politics and Policies of the Truman Administation* (Chicago: Quadrangle Books) (1970)

Beschloss, M., *The Conquerors-Roosevelt, Truman and the Destruction of Hitler's Germany, 1941-1945* (New York and London: Simon & Schuster) (2002)

Betts R.R. (Ed), *Central and South East Europe 1945-1948* (London and New York: Royal Institute of International Affairs) (1950)

Bialer, S., *The Soviet Paradox: External Expansion, Internal Decline* (New York: Knopf) (1986)

Blaxland, G., *Alexander's Generals (the Italian Campaign 1944-1945)* (London: William Kimber & Co) (1979)

Blessing, B., *The Antifascist classroom-Denazification in Soviet-occupied Germany, 1945-1949* (Basingstoke and New York: Palgrave Macmillan) (2006)

Bobbitt, P., *The Shield of Achilles: War, Peace and the Course of History* (London: Allen Lane) (2002)

Bohri, L.:
- *Hungary in the Cold War, 1945-1956 : Between the United States and the Soviet Union* (Budapest and New York: Central European University Press) (2004)
- 'The Merchants of the Kremlin: The Economic Roots of Soviet Expansion in Hungary', Working Paper No. 28, Cold War International History Project Washington, DC, June 2000

Bonnet, H., *The United Nations on the Way: Principles and Policies* (Chicago: World Citizens Association) (1942)

Booth, K. and Smith S., *International Relations Theory Today* (Cambridge: Polity Press:) (1995)

Borkin, J., *The Crime and Punishment of I. G. Farben* (New York: The Free Press) (1978)

Borkin, J. and Welsh, C.A., *Germany's Master Plan: The Story of Industrial Offensive* (New York: Melbourne Long) (1943)

Botting, D., *The Second Front* (Alexandria, Va.: Time-Life Books) (1978)

Bower, T., *The Pledge Betrayed-America and Britain and the Denazification of Post-War Germany* (Garden City, NY: DoubleDay and Co.) (1982)

Brinkley, A., *American History: A Survey* (New York: McGraw-Hill) (1986)

Brivati, B. and Jones, H. (eds.), *From Reconstruction to Integration-Britain and Europe since 1945* (Leicester, London and New York: Leicester University Press) (1993)

Brown, C., *Understanding International Relations* (London and Basingstoke: Palgrave) (2001)

Brown, M. and Lynn-Jones, S. and Miller, S., (ed.), *Debating the Democratic Peace* (Cambridge, MA: MIT Press) (1996)

Buhite, R., *Decisions at Yalta: An Appraisal of Summit Diplomacy* (Wilmington, DE: Scholarly Resources) (1986)

Bull H., *The Anarchical Society* (Basingstoke: Macmillan) (1995)

Bullock, A., *Hitler-A Study in Tyranny* (Harmondsworth, Middx.: Pelican Books Ltd.) (1965)

Burchill S., Linklater A., Devetak R., Paterson M. and True J., (Ed.) *Theories of International Relations*, (London: Macmillan) (1997)

Burchett, W., *Cold War in Germany* (Melbourne: World Unity Publications) (1950)

Burleigh, M., *The Third Reich: A New History.* (Basingstoke: Macmillan) (2000)

Buzan, B.:

- 'The Primary Institutions of International Society', Paper presented at BISA Conference London December 2002
- *From International Society to World Society? English School Theory and the Social Structure of Globalisation* (Cambridge: Cambridge University Press) (2004)
- *The United States and the Great Powers: World Politics in the Twenty First Century* (Oxford and New York: Oxford University Press) (2000)

Buzan, B. and Little R., *International Systems in World History-Remaking the Study of international relations* (Oxford and New York: Oxford University Press) (2000)

Buzan, B., Little, R. and Jones, C, *The Logic of Anarchy: Neorealism to Strcutural Realism* (New York: Columbia University Press) (1993)

Calhoun, C., (ed.), *Dictionary of the Social Sciences* (Oxford and New York: Oxford University Press) (2002)

Calvocoressi, P., *Nüremberg-The facts, the law and the consequences* (London: Chatto & Windus) (1947)

Candeloro, G., *Storia dell'Italia Moderna, Vol. XI* (Milan: Feltrinelli Editori) (1986)

Carver, *The Imperial War Museum Book of the War in Italy 1943-1945* (London: Sidgwick & Jackson) (2001)

Casey, S., 'Franklin D. Roosevelt, Ernest 'Putzi' Hanfstaengl and the 'S-Project', June 1942-June 1944,' *Journal of Contemporary History*, 35, July 2000: 339-59

Childers, T. and Caplan, J. (eds.), *Reevaluating the Third Reich* (New York: Holmes and Meier) (1993)

Clark, C., *Iron Kingdom-The Rise and Downfall of Prussia, 1600-1947* (London: Allen Books, Penguin) (2006)

Claude I., *Swords into Plowshares: The Problems and Progress of International Organization* (London: University of London Press) (1965)

Clarke, R., *Anglo-American Economic Collaboration in War and Peace, 1942-1949* (Oxford: Oxford University Press) (1982)

Cobban, A., *A History of Modern France, Vol. III, 1871-1962*, (Harmondsworth, Middlesex) (1965)

Cordell, H., *The Memoirs of Cordell Hull*, Volume 1 (New York: Macmillan.) (1948)

Coutouvidis, J. and Reynolds, J., *Poland 1939-1947* (Leicester: Leicester University Press) (1986)

Cowley, R., (ed.) *What If? Military Historians Imagine What Might Have Been* (London: Pan Books) (2001)

Crew, D., (ed.) *Nazism and German Society 1933-1945* (London: Routledge) (1994)

Dahrendorf, R., *Society and Democracy in Germany* (London: Weidenfeld and Nicholson) (1965)

Davidson, B., *Germany: What Now? Potsdam 1945-Partition 1949* (London: Frederick Muller Ltd.) (1950)

Davies, N., *Europe: A History* (London: Pimlico) (1997)

Davison, W. P., *The Berlin Blockade: A Study in Cold War Politics* (Princeton: Princeton University Press) (1958)

Dawson, R. H., *The Decision to Aid Russia, 1941: Foreign Policy and Domestic Politics* (University of North Carolina: Chapel Hill) (1959)

Deighton, A., *The Impossible Peace: Britain, the Division of Germany and the Origins of the Cold War* (Oxford: Clarendon) (1990)

De Gaulle et la Nation face aux problèmes de défense (Paris: Plon) (1983)

De Felice, R., *Storia del Fascismo* (Milan: Luce Libero) (2004)

De Long B.J. and Eichengreen B., *The Marshall Plan: History's Most Successful Structural Adjustment Program*, Working Paper no. 3899, National Bureau of Economic Research, Washington DC, October 1991

Der Derian, James, *On Diplomacy. A Genealogy of Western Estrangement* (Oxford: Blackwell) (1987)

Dietrich, J., *The Morgenthau Plan: Soviet Influence on American Postwar Policy* (New York: Algora Publications) (2002)

DiLorenzo, T.J., *How Capitalism Saved America-The Untold History of our Country. From the Pilgrims to the Present* (New York: Three Rivers Press) (2004)

Dobson, Alan P., *U.S. wartime aid to Britain 1940-1946* (London: Croom Helm) (1986)

Dockrill, M., and McKercher, B., (ed.) *Diplomacy and World Power: Studies in British Foreign Policy, 1890-1950* (Cambridge and New York: Cambridge University Press) (1996)

Dorplaen, A.:

- *World of General Haushofer: Geopolitics in Action, 1942* (New York and Toronto: Farrar & Rinehart) (1942)
- *German History in Marxist Perspective: The East German Perspective* (London: IB Tauris & Co. Ltd) (1985)

Dornbusch R., Nölling W., and Layard R., (ed) *Postwar Economic Reconstruction and Lessons for the East Today* (Cambridge, Mass. and London: The MIT Press) (1993)

Dougherty, James J., *The Politics of Wartime Aid: American Economic Assistance to France and French Northwest Africa, 1940-1946* (Westport, Conn. and London: Greenwood Press) (1978)

Doyle, M., *Ways of War and Peace: Realism, Liberalism, and Socialism* (New York: W.W. Norton) (1997)

Duffy, C., *Red Storm on the Reich-The Soviet March on Germany, 1945* (London: Routledge) (1991)

Dunne T.:
- 'The Social Construction of International Society', *European Journal of International Relations*, 1:3 (1995)
- *Inventing International Society: A History of the English School* (New York: St. Martin's Press, in association with St. Antony's College, Oxford) (1998)

Ebsworth, R., *Restoring Democracy in Germany: The British Contribution* (London: Stevens & Sons) (1960)

Eichelberger, C., *Organizing for Peace: A Personal History of the Founding of the United Nations* (New York and London: Harper and Row) (1977)

Eisenberg, C. W., *Drawing the Line: The American Decision to Divide Germany, 1944-1949* (Cambridge: Cambridge University Press) (1996)

Eley, G., *Forging Democracy: The History of the Left in Europe, 1850-2000* (Oxford and New York: Oxford University Press) (2002)

Evans G., and Newnham J., (Ed.) *Penguin Dictionary of International Relations* (London: Penguin Books) (1998)

Falk, R., Kratochwil, F. and Mendlovitz S., (ed) *International Law: A Contemporary Perspective* (Boulder, CO and London: Westview Press) (1985)

Feis, H., *From Trust to Terror: The Onset of the Cold War, 1945-50* (London: Blond) (1970)

Frei, N., *National Socialist Rule in Germany: The Führer State 1933-1945*, (Oxford: Blackwell) (1993)

Fischer, L., *The Road to Yalta* (New York: Harper & Row) (1972)

Ferro, M., *The Great War 1914-1918* (London and New York: Routledge) (2002)

Fest, J., *Hitler* (London: Penguin Books) (2002)

Finkelstein, N. and Birn, R. B., *A Nation on Trial-The Goldhagen Thesis and Historical Truth* (New York: An Owl Book-Henry Holt and Company) (1998)

Fischer, K., *Storia della Germania Nazista-Nascita e decandenza del Terzo Reich* (Newton and Compton: Rome) (2001)

Fitz Gibbon, C., *Denazification* (London: Joseph) (1969)

Flanagan, C., and Taberner, S., *1949/1989: Cultural Perspectives on Division and Unity in East and West* (Amsterdam and Atlanta, GA: German Monitor no. 50, Editions Rodopi B.V.) (1994)

Fleming, D. F., *The Cold War and its Origins, 1917-1960*, 2 vols. (New York: Allen and Unwin) (1961)

Fleming, T., *The New Dealers' War: F.D.R. And The War Within World War Two* (New York: Basic Books) (2001)

Foerster, F. W., *Europe and the German Question* (London: George Allen & Unwin) (1941)

Fordham, B. O., 'Economic Interests, Party, and Ideology in Early Cold War Era: U.S. Foreign Policy', *International Organization, Vol. 52, No. 2, Spring, 1998*

Forrestal, J., *The Forrestal Diaries*, ed. Walter Millis and Duffield E.S. (New York: Viking Press) (1951)

Fox, W. T.R., *The Super-Powers: The United States, Britain, and the Soviet Union: Their Responsibility for Peace* (New York: Harcourt, Brace & Co.) (1944)

Freeden, M., *The New Liberalism: An Ideology of Social Reform* (Oxford: Clarendon Press) (1978)

Frost. M., *Towards a Normative Theory of International Relations* (Cambridge. Cambridge University Press) (1986)

Funk, W., *Verein Berliner Kaufleute und Industrieller und Wirtschafts-Hochschule Berlin* (Ed.), Europäische Wirtschaftsgemeinschaft (Berlin: Haude & Spenersche Verlagsbuchhandlung Max Paschke) (1943)

Gaddis Lewis, J.:

- *Strategies of Containment: A Critical Appraisal of Postwar American National Security Policy* (Oxford and New York: OUP) (1982)
- *We Now Know: Rethinking Cold War History* (Oxford: Clarendon) (1997)
- *The United States and the Origins of the Cold War, 1941-1947* (New York: Columbia University Press) (1972)
- *Strategies of Containment* (New York: Oxford University Press) (1982)
- 'The Emerging Post-Revisionist Synthesis on the Origins of the Cold War', *Diplomatic History* 7, Summer 1983
- *Long Peace* (Oxford an New York: Oxford University Press) (1987)

Gaddis Lewis, J. and Deibel, T., *Containing the Soviet Union: A Critique of U.S. Policy* (Washington, D.C. and London: Pergamon-Brassey's International Defense) (1987)

Gardner, L., *Architects of Illusion. Men and Ideas in American Foreign Policy, 1941-1949* (Chicago: Quadrangle Books) (1970)

Garthoff, R.:

- *Soviet Military Doctrine* (Glencoe, Illinois: The Free Press) (1953)
- 'The Concept of the Balance of Power in Soviet Policy Making', *World Politics,* October 1951

Ghods, M. Reza, *Iran in the Twentieth Century: a Political History*, (Boulder, CO: Lynne Rienner Publishers) (1989)

Gimbel, J., *The Origins of the Marshall Plan* (Stanford, CA: Stanford University Press) (1976)

Gong, G., *The Standard of 'Civilization' in International Society* (Oxford: Clarendon Press) (1984)

Gordon, J.S., *The Empire of Wealth-The Epic History of the American Economic Power* (New York, London, Toronto, Sydney: Harper Perennial) (2005)

Gormly, J., *From Potsdam to the Cold War: Big Three Diplomacy, 1945-1947* (Wilmington, Del: SR Books) (1990)

Gori, F., and Pons S. (Ed.), *The Soviet Union and Europe in the Cold War 1943-53* (Basingstoke and New York: Palgrave MacMillan) (1996)

Gottlieb., M., *The German Peace Settlement and the Berlin Crisis* (New Brunswick, N.J.: Transaction Inc) (1960)

Greenwood S., *Britain and the Cold War, 1945-1991* (Houndmills, England: Macmillan Press; New York: St. Martin's Press) (2000)

Goldhagen, D. J., *Hitler's Willing Executioners-Ordinary Germans and the Holocaust* (London: Little, Brown and Company) (1996)

Grogin R.,. *Natural Enemies-the United States and the Soviet Union in the Cold War, 1917-1991* (Lanham, Md.: Lexington Books) (2000)

Gulick, E. V., *Europe's Classical Balance of Power: A Case History of the Theory and Practice of One of the Great Concepts of European Statecraft* (London and New York: Norton) (1955)

Guth, S., *Les Forces Françaises en Allemagne : La Citadelle Utopique* (Paris: Editions l'Hartmann) (1991)

Haas, M, *International Conflict* (Indianapolis: Bobs-Merrill) (1974)

Hahn, H.J., *Education and Society in Germany* (Oxford and Providence: Berg Publishers) (1998)

Halle, L., *The Cold War as History* (New York: Harper and Row) (1967)

Harms K., Lutz R. Reuter and Volker Durr, *Coping with the Past: Germany and Austria after 1945* (London: University of Wisconsin Press) (1991)

Hansen, J., *Correlation of Forces: Four Decades of Soviet Military Development* (London and New York: Praeger Publishers) (1987)

Hardach, K., *The Political Economy of Germany in the Twentieth Century* (Berkeley, Los Angeles, London: University of California Press) (1980)

Hastings, M.:

- *Overlord-D-Day and the Battle for Normandy* (New York and Sydney: Pan Books) (1984)
- *Armageddon: The Battle for Germany 1944-45* (London: MacMillan) (2004)
- *Bomber Command* (London: Pan MacMillan) (1999)

Hearnden, A. (ed.), *The British in Germany: Educational Reconstruction after 1945* (London: Hamilton) (1978)

Herring Jr, George C., *Aid to Russia, 1941-6: Strategy, Diplomacy and Origins of the Cold War* (London and New York: Columbia University Press) (1973)
Heske, H., 'Karl Haushofer: His Role in German Politics and in Nazi Politics', *Political Geography* 6 (1987)
Higgins H., *The Cold War* (London: Heinemann Educational Books) (1984)
Higham, C, *Trading with the Enemy-An Exposé of the Nazi-American Money Plot, 1933-1949* (London: Robert Hale) (1983)
Hillel, M, *L'Occupation Francaise en Allemagne* (Paris: Balland) (1983)
Hitchcock, W., *France Restored: Cold War Diplomacy and the Quest for Leadership in Europe, 1944-1954* (Chapel Hill: University of North Carolina Press) (1998)
Hitchins, K., *Rumania, 1866-1947* (Oxford: Clarendon Press) (1994)
Hoffman, P.:
- *Stauffenberg: A Family History, 1905-1944* (Cambridge: Cambridge University Press) (1995)
- *Stauffenberg und der 20. Juli 1944* (München: C.H.Beck) (1998)

Hogan M., *The Marshall Plan: America, Britain, and the Reconstruction of Western Europe, 1947-1952* (Cambridge: Cambridge University Press) (1987)
Holm H.H. and Sørensen G. (eds.), *Whose World Order*? Uneven Globalization and the End of the Cold War (Boulder, CO: Westview Press) (1995)
Holsti, K., *Peace and War: Armed Conflict and International Order 1648-1989* (Cambridge: Cambridge University Press) (1991)
Horowitz, D.:
- (ed.), *Containment and Revolution: Western Policy towards Social Revolution: 1917 to Vietnam* (London: Blond) (1967)
- *The Free World Colossus: A Critique of American Foreign Policy during the Cold War* (London: MacGibbon and Kee) (1965)

Hughes, R. G,. *Britain, Germany and the Cold War: The Search for a European Détente 1949-1967* (Abingdon, Oxon: Routledge) (2007)

Iakovlev, A.N., *The Yalta Conference 1945: Lessons of History* (Moscow: Novosti Press Agency) (1985)

Ikenberry, G.J., *After Victory: Institutions, Strategic Restraint, and the Rebuilding of Order after Major Wars* (Princeton, N.J.: Princeton University Press) (2001)

Ireland, T., *Creating the Entangling Alliance* (Westport, Conn.: Greenwood Press) (1981)

Jackson, R.:

- *The Global Covenant: Human Conduct in a World of States* (Oxford: Oxford University Press) (2000)
- 'Pluralism in International Political Theory', *Review of International Studies*, 18 (1992)

James, A.:

- 'The Practice of Sovereign Statehood in Contemporary International Society', *Political Studies* (1999) 47 (3): 468
- (ed.), *The Bases of International Order: Essays in Honour of C. A. W. Manning* (London: Oxford University Press) (1973)

Jarausch, K. and Duffy, E., *Dictatorship as Experience: Towards a Socio-Cultural History of the GDR* (Oxford and Providence, NI: Berghahn Books) (1999)

Johnson, C., *An Instance of Treason: The Story of Tokyo Spy Ring* (London: William Heinemann Ltd.) (1965)

Jukes G., *The Development of Soviet Strategic Thinking since* 1945 (Canberra: Australian National University Press) (1972)

Kant, I., *Perpetual Peace: A Philosophical Sketch:* http://www.mtholyoke.edu/acad/intrel/kant/kant1.htm

Kennan, G., *Realities of American Foreign Policy* (Princeton: Princeton University Press) (1954)

Kennedy, D., *Freedom from Want: The American People in Depression and War 1929-1945* (Oxford and New York: Oxford University Press) (1999)

Kennedy-Pipe, C., *Stalin's Cold War: Soviet Strategies in Europe, 1943 to 1956* (Manchester: Manchester University Press) (1995)

Kershaw, I., *The Nazi Dictatorship: Problems and Perspectives of Interpretation* (London: Arnold) (2000)

Kimball, W.:

- *Swords or Ploughshares? The Morgenthau Plan for Defeat Nazi Germany, 1943-1946* (Philadelphia and New York: J.B. Lippincott Co.) (1976)
- *The Most Unsordid Act: Lend-Lease, 1939-1941* (Baltimore, MD: Johns Hopkins University) (1969)

Kirkendall, R., (ed) *The Truman Period as a Research Field* (Columbia: University of Missouri Press) (1967)

Kirkpatrick, C, *An unknown Future and a Doubtful Present: Writing the Victory Plan of 1941* (Washington, D.C.: Center of Military History, United States Army) (1990)

Kissinger, H., *The Necessity for Choice: Prospects of American Foreign Policy* (London: Chatto and Windus) (1961)

Klafkowski, A., *The Potsdam Agreement* (Warsaw: Panatwowe Wydawnictwo Naukowe) (1963)

Knudsen, T. B., (1999) *Humanitarian Intervention and International Society: Contemporary manifestations of an explosive doctrine* (manus, 432 pp.), (Aarhus: Department of Political Science, University of Aarhus)

Kolko, G.:

- 'American Business and Germany, 1930-1941', *The Western Political Quarterly,* Volume XV, (1962)
- *The Politics of War-Allied Diplomacy of the World Crisis of 1943-1945* (London: Weidenfeld and Nicholson) (1969)

Kolko, G. and Kolko, J., *The Limits of Power: The World and U.S. Foreign Policy, 1945–1954* (New York: Harper and Row) (1972)

Kostrzewa, W., 'A Marshall Plan for Middle and Eastern Europe', *World Economy 13* (March 1990), pp. 27-49

Kratochwil, F., *Rules, Norms and Decisions: On the Conditions of Practical and Legal Reasoning in International Relations and Domestic Affairs* (Cambridge: Cambridge University Press) (1989)

Krisch H., *German Politics under Soviet Occupation* (New York: Columbia University Press) (1974)

Kuklick, B., *American Policy and the Division of Germany: The Clash with Russia over Reparations* (Ithaca and London: Cornell University Press) (1972)

Kuniholm, B., *The Origins of the Cold War in the Near East* (Princeton: Princeton University Press) (1987)

LaFeber, W.:

- (Ed.), *The Origins of the Cold War, 1941-1947: A Historical Problems with Interpretations and Documents* (New York and Chichester: Wiley) (1971)
- *America, Russia, and the Cold War, 1945-1992* (New York and London: McGraw-Hill) (1993)

Lambert, P., 'German Historians and Nazi ideology: The Parameters of the Volksgemeinschaft and the Problems of Historical Legitimation', *European History Quarterly* 25, 1995. pp. 555-82

Langhorne, K. and R., *The Practice of Diplomacy: Its Evolution, Theory and Administration* (London: Routledge) (1995)

Leffler, M.:

- 'The Struggle for Germany and the Origins of the Cold War', Occasional Paper No. 16, German Historical Institute (Washington, DC)
- *A Preponderance of Power: National Security, the Truman Administration, and the Cold War* (Stanford: Stanford University Press) (1992)

Lebow, R.N., *Between Peace and War-The Nature of International Crisis* (Baltimore: The John Hopkins University Press) (1981)

Lebra, J., C., (ed.) *Japan's Greater East Asia Co-Prosperity Sphere in World War II: Selected Readings and Documents* (Oxford: Oxford University Press) (1975)

Lewkowicz, N., 'The German Question and the International Order (1943-8)': www.leeds.ac.uk/polis/englishschool/lewkowiczo5.doc)

Levy, C. and Roseman, M. (eds), *Three Postwar Eras in Comparison-Western Europe 1918-1945-1989* (Basingstoke and New York: Palgrave) (2002)

Lider, J., *Correlation of Forces: An Analysis of Marxist-Leninist Concepts* (Gower: Aldershot) (1986)

Linklater, A., *The Transformation of Political Community: Ethical Foundations of the Post-Westphalian Era* (Columbia: University of South Carolina Press) (1998)

Loewenthal, F., *News from Soviet Germany* (London: Gollancz) (1950)

Loth W., *Stalin's Unwanted Child: The Soviet Union, the German Question and the Founding of the GDR* (Houndmills, Basingstoke: Macmillan Press) (1998)

L'Ouvre Culturelle Française en Allemagne (Paris: Impremerie Nationale) (1947)

Luard, E., *A History of the United Nations*, Vol. I (London and Basingstoke: MacMillan Ltd) (1982)

Lukacs, J.:

- *The Hitler of History-Hitler's Biographers on Trial* (London: Phoenix Press) (1997)
- *The Great Powers and Eastern Europe* (New York: American Book Co.) (1953)

Lucas, S., *Freedom's War: The US Crusade against the Soviet Union, 1945-56* (Manchester: Manchester University Press) (1999)

Lundestad, G.:

- *The American Non-Policy Towards Eastern Europe 1943-1947* (Tromsö, Oslo, Bergen: Universiteitsforlaget) (1978)
- 'Empire by Invitation? The United States and Europe, 1945-1952', *Journal of Peace Research* 23, no. 3 (1986): 263-77
- *'Empire' by Integration: The United States and European Integration, 1945-1997* (New York: Oxford University Press) (1998)

Lynch M., *Stalin and Khrushchev: The USSR, 1924-64* (London: Hodder & Stoughton) (1990)

Machiavelli, N,. *The Prince* (London: Dent) (1958)

Mark, E.:

- 'Charles E. Bohlen and the Limits of Soviet Hegemony in Eastern Europe', *Diplomatic History* 3:2 (Spring 1979)
- 'American Policy Towards Eastern Europe and the Origins of the Cold War, 1941-1946: An Alternative Explanation', *Journal of American History* 68 (September 1981)

McCormick, T., *America's Half Century* (Baltimore: Johns Hopkins University Press) (1989)

Macdonald, D. J., 'Communist Bloc Expansion in the Early Cold War: Challenging Realism, Refuting Revisionism', *International Security,* Vol. 20, no. 3 (Winter 1995)

Macmillan, M., *Peacemakers: The Paris Peace Conference of 1919 and Its Attempt to End War* (London: John Murray) (2001)

Maddox, R.:

- *The New Left and the Origins of the Cold War* (Princeton: Princeton University Press) (1973)
- *The Senatorial Career of Harley Martin Kilgore* (New York: Garland Publishing Company) (1981)

Maier, C., 'Revisionism and the Interpretation of Cold War Origins, Perspectives', *American History* 4 (1970)

Mark, E., 'Revolution By Degrees: Stalin's National-Front Strategy For Europe, 1941-1947', The Cold War International History Project Working Paper, no. 31

Marshall, B., *The Origins of Post-War German Politics* (London, New York, Sydney: Croom Helm) (1988)

Martel, Leon, *Lend-lease, Loans, and the Coming of the Cold War: A Study of the Implementation of Foreign Policy* (Boulder, CO: Westview Press) (1979)

Martel, G., (ed.), *American Foreign Relations Reconsidered, 1890-1993* (London: Routledge) (1994)

Mastny, V.:
- *Russia's Road to the cold War-Diplomacy, Warfare, and the Politics of Communism, 1941-5* (New York: Columbia University Press) (1979)
- *The Cold War and Soviet Insecurity* (New York: Oxford University Press) (1996)

Mattern, J., *Geopolitik: Doctrine of National Self-Sufficiency and Empire* (Baltimore: The Johns Hopkins Press) (1942)

Matloff, M. and Snell, E., *Strategic Planning for Coalition Warfare 1941-1942* (Washington D.C.: Office of the Chief of Military History, Department of the Army) (1953)

Mayall, J., *World Politics: Progress and its Limits* (Cambridge: Polity Press) (2000)

Mayle, Paul D., *Eureka Summit: Agreement in Principle and the Big Three at Tehran, 1943* (Newark: University of Delaware Press; London: Associated University Presses) (1987)

Mazower, M., *Dark Continent: Europe's Twentieth Century* (London: Allen Lane) (1998)

McAllister, J., *No Exit: America and the German Problem, 1943-1954* (Ithaca: Cornell University Press) (2002)

McCauley, M., *The German Democratic Republic since 1945* (London and Basingstoke: The Macmillan Press:) (1983)

McCoy, A. W., *Southeast Asia under Japanese Occupation* (New Haven, CT: Yale University SE Asian Studies) (1980)

McGuigan, R., *The Allied Occupation Army in Post-Waterloo France* (Napoleon Series) http://www.napoleon-series.org

McMahon, R., *The Cold War on the Periphery* (New York: Columbia University Press) (1994)

Mee, C.L., *Meeting at Potsdam* (London: Book Club Edition) (1975)

Meinecke, F., *The German Catastrophe: Reflections and Recollections* (Harvard, MA: Harvard University Press) (1950)

Merridale, C., *Ivan's War: The Red Army 1939-1945* (London: Faber and Faber) (2005)

Merrit, *Democracy Imposed: U.S. Occupation Policy and the German Public, 1945-1949* (New Haven and London: Yale University Press) (1995)

Milward, A.S., *The Reconstruction of Western Europe, 1945-1951* (London: Methuen) (1984)

Miller R.:

- (Ed.), *The Evolution of the Cold War from Confrontation to Containment* (New York and London:_Holt, Rinehart and Winston) (1972)
- *To Save a City: The Berlin Airlift, 1948-1949* (College Station, TX: Texas A&M University Press) (2000),

Milward, A.S., *The Reconstruction of Western Europe, 1945-1951* (London: Methuen) (1984)

Mitchell, O., *The Cold War in Germany-Overview, Origins and Intelligence Wars* (Lanham, MD: University Press of America) (2005)

Mitrany, David, *The Functional Theory of Politics* (London: Martin Robinson & Co.) (1975)

Montgomery, J.D., *Forced to be Free: The Artificial Revolution in Germany and Japan* (Chicago: Chicago University Press) (1957)

Moorhouse R., *Killing Hitler*: *The Plots, the Assassins, and the Dictator Who Cheated Death* (New York: Bantam Books (2006)

Moreton E., *Germany between East and West* (Cambridge: Cambridge University Press/RIIA) (1987)

Morgenthau, H.:

- (Ed.), *Germany and the Future of Europe* (Chicago: University of Chicago) (1951)
- *Politics Among Nations: The Struggle for Power and Peace* (London and New York: McGraw Hill (1993)

Morley, J. W. (ed). *Japan's Road to the Pacific War. The Fateful Choice: Japan's Advance into Southeast Asia, 1939-1941* (New York: Columbia University Press) (1980)

Mosely, P. E.:
- 'The Dismemberment of Germany-Allied Negotiations from Yalta to Potsdam', *Foreign Affairs* (April, 1950)
- *The Kremlin and World Politics* (New York: Vintage Books) (1960)

Mueller, J., *Retreat from Doomsday*: *The Obsolescence of Major War* (New York, Woodbridge: University of Rochester Press) (1996)

Muhlen, N., *The Return of Germany: A Tale of Two Countries* (London: The Bodley Head) (1953)

Munk, F., *The Legacy of Nazism: The Economic and Social Consequences of Totalitarism* (New York: The MacMillan Company) (1943)

Mykołayczyk, S., *The Rape of Poland*: *Pattern of Soviet Aggression* (New York: Whittlesey House) (1948)

Naimark, N., *The Russians in Germany: A History of the Soviet Zone of Occupation, 1945-1949* (Cambridge, MA and London: The Belknap Press of Harvard University Press)

Nardin T.:
- *Law, Morality and the Relations of States* (Princeton, NJ.: Princeton University Press) (1983)
- (with Mapel, D.) (ed), *International Society: Diverse Ethical Perspectives* (Princeton, N.J.: Princeton University Press) (1998)

Nettl, J.P., *Eastern Zone and Soviet Policy in Germany 1945-50* (Oxford: Oxford University Press) (1951)

Neumann, F., *Behemoth: The Structure and Practice of National Socialism* (London: Victor Gollancz Ltd.) (1942)

Neumann, W., *Making The Peace 1941-5-The Diplomacy of the Wartime Conferences* (Washington, D.C: Foundation for Foreign Affairs) (1950)

Nicholls, A.J., *Weimar and the Rise of Hitler* (London: Mac Millan-St. Martin Press) (1968)

Niebuhr, R., *The Nature and Destiny of Man: A Christian Interpretation* (London: Nisbet) (1941-3)

Noakes, J and Pridham, G (ed.), *A Documentary Reader: Nazism 1919-1945, Vol 2, State, Economy and Society 1933-1939* (Exeter: University of Exeter Press) (2000)

Northedge, F.S., *Descent from Power: British Foreign Policy 1945-1973* (London: George Allen and Unwin Ltd) (1974)

Oakeshott M., *On Human Conduct* (Oxford: Clarendon) (1990)

Oppenheim, L., *International. Law: A Treatise* (London, 1920-21), online edition: http://gallica.bnf.fr/ark:/12148/bpt6k93562g and http://gallica.bnf.fr/ark:/12148/bpt6k93563t

Orgill, D., *The Gothic Line (The Autumn Campaign in Italy 1944)* (London: Heinemann) (1967)

Overy, R.,:

- *Why the Allies Won* (London: Pimlico) (1995)
- *The Dictators: Hitler's Germany and Stalin's Russia* (London: Pimlico) (1995)
- 'Class and Community in the Third Reich', *Historical Journal* 22, 1979

Owen, J, *The Nuremberg Trials: Evil on Trial* (London: Review) (2006)

Parrish S. D. and Narinsky M., 'New Evidence on the Soviet Rejection of the Marshall Plan, 1947: Two Reports', Cold War International History Project, Washington, DC, 1994

Paterson, T., *Soviet-American Confrontation: Postwar Reconstruction and the Origins of the Cold War* (Baltimore and London: Johns Hopkins University Press) (1973)

Pechatnov, V., *The Big Three after World War Two: New Documents about Post-war Soviet Relations with the United States and Great Britain* (Washington, DC: Cold War International History Project) (1995)

Penrose, E.F., *Economic Planning for the Peace* (Princeton, NJ: Princeton University Press) (1953)

Perlmutter, A., *FDR and Stalin: A Not So Grand Alliance,* 1943-1945 (Columbia & London: University of Missouri Press) (1993)

Persico, J., *Nuremberg: Infamy on Trial* (New York and London: Penguin Books) (1994)

Pechatnov V. and Earl Edmonson C., *Debating the Origins of the Cold War: American and Russian Perspectives (Debating Twentieth-Century America)* (Lanham, MD: Rowman & Littlefield Publishers) (2002)

Penrose, E.F., *Economic Planning for the Peace* (Princeton: Princeton University Press) (1953)

Peterson, E.N.:

- *The American Occupation of Germany-Retreat to Victory* (Detroit: Wayne State University Press) (1977)
- *Soviet-American Confrontation* (Baltimore: Johns Hopkins University Press) (1973)

Peukert, D J K., *Inside Nazi Germany: Conformity, Opposition and Racism in Everyday Life* (London: Batsford) (1987)

Phillips , A. L. *Soviet Policy toward East Germany Reconsidered: The Postwar Decade* (Westport, CT: Greenwood Press) (1986)

Picknett, L., Prince, C. and Prior, S., Brydon, R., *Double Standards: The Rudolph Hess Cover Up* (London: Paperback) (2001)

Plischke, E., 'History of the Allied High Commission for Germany: Its Establishment, Structure and Procedures', Research Project no. 107. Historical Division, Office of the Executive Secretary, Office of U.S. High Commissioner for Germany (1951)

Poidevin, R., 'La France et le Charbon allemande au lendemain de la deuxième guerre mondiale', *Relations Internationales*, no. 44, hiver 1985

Polanyi, K., *The Great Transformation* (Boston, MA: Beacon Press) (1957)

Pollard, R., *Economic Security and the Origins of the Cold War, 1945-1950* (New York: Columbia University Press) (1985)

Polonsky A. and Drukier, B (eds.), *The Beginnings of Communist Rule in Poland* (London: Routledge and Kegan Paul) (1980)

Pritchard, G., *The Making of the GDR 1945-53: From Antifascism to Stalinism* (Manchester and New York: Manchester University Press) (2000)

Raack, R. C., *Stalin's Drive to the West, 1938-1945* (Stanford: Stanford University Press) (1995)

Ratchford, B.U and Ross, WM.D., *Berlin Reparations Assignment: Round One of the German Peace Settlement* (Chapel Hill, NC: University of North Carolina Press) (1947)

Reeves, J., 'International Society and International Law', *American Journal of International Law*, Volume 15, Issue 3 (July 1921)

Reus-Smit, C., (1997) 'The Constitutional Structure of International Society and the Nature of Fundamental Institutions', *International Organization*, 51 (4): 555-89

Reynolds, D.:

- *Rich Relations: The American Occupation of Britain 1942-1945* (London: Harper Collins Publishers) (1996)
- *The Origins of the Cold War in Europe: International Perspectives* (London: Yale University Press) (1994)
- *The Creation of the Anglo-American Alliance 1937-1941: A Study on Competitive Cooperation* (London: Europa) (1981)

Richardson, J. L., 'Cold War Revisionism', *World Politics* 24 (1972): 579-612

Richter, W., *Re-educating Germany* (Chicago, IL: University of Chicago Press) (1945)

Rizi, F. F., *Benedetto Croce and Italian Fascism* (Toronto: University of Toronto Press) (2003)

Roberts, G.:

- 'History and IR', *Review of International Studies*, Volume 32 Number 4 October 2006
- *Stalin's Wars: From World War to Cold War 1939-1953* (New Haven, CT and London: Yale University Press) (2006),

Rodnick, D., *Postwar Germans: An Anthropological's Account* (New Haven: Yale University Press) (1948)

Roger, W.L., *Imperialism at Bay, 1941-1945: The United States and the Decolonization of the British Empire* (Oxford: Clarendon Press) (1977)

Rosenthal, Joel H., *Ethics & International Affairs: A Reader* (Washington, D.C.: Georgetown University Press) (1999)

Rostow, W.W., *The Division of Europe After World War II: 1946* (Lawrence, KS: Kansas University Press) (1972)

Rothschild, J., *Return to Diversity: A Political History of East Central Europe* (New York and Oxford: OUP) (1993)

Ruotsila M., *British and American Anticommunism before the Cold War* (London and Portland, OR: Frank Cass) (2001)

Sainsbury, K., *The Turning Point: Roosevelt, Stalin, Churchill, and Chiang-Kai-Shek, 1943: the Moscow, Cairo and Teheran Conferences* (Oxford: Oxford University Press) (1985)

Samuel R.H. and R. Hinton Thomas, *Education and Society in Modern Germany* (London: Routledge & Kegan Paul) (1949)

Schaffer, G., *Russian Zone* (London: Published for the Co-operative Press by George Allen & Unwin) (1947)

Schlesinger, A., 'Origins of the Cold War', *Foreign Affairs* 46, no. 1 (October 1967)

Schmitt C., *The Concept of the Political* (Chicago: University of Chicago Press) (1996)

Schwartz T., *America's Germany* (Cambridge: Harvard University Press) (1991)

Sharp, T., *The Wartime Alliance and the Zonal Division of Germany* (Oxford: Clarendon Press) (1975)

Sherwood, R., *Roosevelt and Hopkins: An Intimate History* (New York: Harper & Brothers) (1948)

Shlaim, A..

- 'The Partition of Germany and the Origins of the Cold War', *Review of International Studies* (1985)
- *The United States and the Berlin Blockade, 1948-1949: A Study in Crisis Decision-making* (Berkeley: University of California Press)(1982)

Shoup, L and Minter, W., *Imperial Brain Trust: The Council on Foreign Relations and the United States Foreign Policy* (New York, Lincoln, NE and Shanghai: Author Choice Press) (1977)

Simhony, A., (ed) *The New Liberalism: Reconciling Liberty and Community* (Cambridge: Cambridge University Press) (2001)

Smith S., Booth, K., Zalewski M. (Ed.), *International Theory: Positivism and Beyond* (Cambridge, New York: Cambridge University Press) (1996)

Smith, N., *American Empire: Roosevelt's Geographer and the Prelude to Globalization* (Berkeley, CA and London: University of California Press) (2003)

Smyser, W R, *From Yalta to Berlin: The Cold War Struggle over Germany* (New York: St. Martin's Press) (1999)

Snell, J. (Ed), *The Meaning of Yalta: Big Three Diplomacy and the New Balance of Power* (Baton Rouge: Lousiana State University) (1956)

Steninger, R. *The German Question: The Stalin Note of 1952 and the Problem of Reunification* (New York: Columbia University) (1990)

Stern, C. and Winkler, H. A., (eds) *Wendepunkte deutscher Geschichte 1848-1990* (Frankfurt: Fischer Taschenbuch Verlag) (1994)

Stoler M. and Gustafson M. (Ed.), *Major Problems in the History of World War Two* (Boston and New York: Houghton Mifflin Co.) (2003)

Solzhenitsyn, A., *Détente: Prospects for Democracy and Dictatorship* (New Brunswick, N.J: Transaction Books) (1980)

Sontheimer, K., *The Government and Politics of West Germany* (London: Hutchinson University Library) (1972)

Spanier, J., *American Foreign Policy Since the World War II* (New York: Praeger) (1973)

Stalin, J., *Speeches Delivered at Meetings of Voters of the Stalin Electoral District* (Moscow: Foreign Languages Publishing House) (1950)

Stimson H. and Bundy, M., *On Active Service in Peace and War* (New York: Harper & Brothers) (1948)

Taubman, W., *Stalin's American Policy* (New York: W. W. Norton) (1982)

Taylor, A J P., *The Course of German History* (London: Methuen & Co) (1978)

Taylor, P. and Groom, A.J.R., *International Institutions at Work* (London: Pinter Publishers Ltd.) (1990)

Temperley, H. and Lane, A. (Ed.), *The Rise and Fall of the Grand Alliance, 1941-1945* (Basingstoke: Macmillan) (1995)

Thomas, H., *Armed Truce* (London: Hamilton) (1986)

Thomas, N., *A Compromised Policy: Britain, Germany and the Soviet Threat 1945-1946* (London, Washington, Montreux: Minerva Press) (1994)

Thompson E. P., *Beyond the Cold War* (London : Merlin Press) (1982)

Tipton, F. B., *A History of Modern Germany Since 1815* (Berkeley and Los Angeles: University of California Press) (2003)

Torriani, R., *Nazis into Germans: Re-education and Democratisation in the British and French Zones of Occupation, 1945-1949*, Ph.D. Thesis (Cambrdige) (2005)

Trachtenberg, M.:

- *A Constructed Peace: The Making of the European Settlement, 1945-1963* (Princeton, N.J.: Princeton University Press) (1999)
- *History and Strategy* (Princeton: Princeton University Press) (1991)

Trent, J., *Mission on the Rhine-Re-education and Denazification in American-Occupied Germany* (Chicago: Chicago University Press) (1982)

Tucker, R., *The Radical Left and American Foreign Policy* (Baltimore: Johns Hokpins University Press) (1971)

Turner, H., *German Big Business and the Rise of Hitler* (New York: Oxford University Press)(1985)

Turner, I (Ed), *Reconstruction in Post-War Germany-British Occupation Policy and the Western Zones 1945-55* (London, New York, Munich: Berg Publishers Ltd.) (1989)

Ulam, A.:

- *The Rivals: America and Russia since World War II* (New York: Viking) (1971)
- *Expansion and Coexistence* (New York: Holt, Rinehart and Winston) (1973)

Vaillant, J., (ed.) *La Denazification par les Vainqueurs : La Politique Culturelle des Occupants en Allemagne 1945-1949* (Lille: Presses Universitaires de Lille) (1981)

Verblen, T., *Imperial Germany and the Industrial Revolution* (New York: B. W. Huebsch) (1918)

Veve, T. D., *The Duke of Wellington and the British Army of Occupation in France, 1815-1818* (Westport, Conn. and London: Greenwood Press) (1992)

Vincent, R.J.:

- *Human Rights and International Relations: Issues and Responses* (Cambridge: Cambridge University Press) (1986)
- *Nonintervention and International Order* (Princeton: Princeton University Press) (1974)

Von Oppen, B., (ed), *Documents of Germany under Occupation 1945-1954* (London: Oxford University Press) (1955)

Wæver, O., 'Does the English School's Via Media Equal the Contemporary Constructivist Middle Ground?', Manchester, BISA Conference Paper, (1999)

Wala, M., *The Council on the Foreign Relations and American Foreign Policy in the Early Cold War* (Providence: Berghahn Books) (1994)

Wallace, M., *American Axis: Henry Ford, Charles Lindbergh, and the Rise of the Third Reich* (New York: St. Martin's Press) (2003)

Walko, John W.. *The Balance of Empires: United States' Rejection of German Reunification and Stalin's March Note of 1952* (Boca Raton, FL: Universal Publishers) (2003)

Waltz, K., *Theory of International Politics* (Boston, MA: McGraw Hill) (1979)

Walzer, M., *Just and Unjust Wars: A Moral Argument with Historical Illustrations* (London: Allen Lane) (1978)

Watson, A., *The Expansion of International Society* (Oxford: Clarendon Press) (1984)

Weiss, S. L.; *The President's Man: Leo Crowley and Franklin Roosevelt in Peace and War* (Carbondale: Southern Illinois University Press) (1996)

Wendt, A.:
- 'Anarchy Is What the States Make of it: The Social Construction of Power Politics', *International Organization* 46, 2, Spring 1992
- *Social Theory of International Politics* (Cambridge and New York: Cambridge University Press) (1999)

Werth, A.:
- *Russia at War 1941-1945* (London: Pan Books Ltd.) (1964)
- *De Gaulle: A Political Biography* (Harmondsworth, Middx.: Penguin Books) (1965)

Westad, O. A., (ed) *Reviewing the Cold War: Approaches, Interpretations, Theory* (London and Portland, OR: Frank Cass) (2000)

Wheeler, N. J.:
- *Saving Strangers: Humanitarian Intervention in International Society* (Oxford: Oxford University Press) (2000)
- 'Pluralist or Solidarist Conceptions of Humanitarian Intervention: Bull and Vincent on Humanitarian Intervention', *Millenium*, Journal of International Studies, 21/2 (1992)

Wheeler-Bennett, J. and Nicholls, A..J., *The Semblance of Peace: The Political Settlement after the Second World War* (London: Macmillan) (1972)

Wheeler-Bennett, J. and Overy, R., *The Nemesis of Power: German Army in Politics, 1918-1945* (New York: Palgrave Macmillan Publishing Company) (1968)

Whiteclay Chambers II, J., (ed.), *The Oxford Companion to American Military History* (Oxford and New York: Oxford University Press) (1999)

Wight M.:
- *International Theory* (London: Leicester University Press) (1991)
- *Power Politics* (New York: Leicester University Press) (1995)

Wight, M. and Butterfield, H. (Ed.), *Diplomatic Investigations: Essays in the Theory of International Politics* (London: George Allen and Unwin) (1966)

Williams, J., 'Pluralism, Solidarism and the Emergence of World Society in English School Theory', *International Relations*, 19:1, (2005)

Williams, W, *The Tragedy of American Diplomacy* (Cleveland and New York: World Publishing Co.) (1959)

Willis, F.R.:

- *The French in Germany 1945-9* (Stanford, CA: Stanford University Press) (1962)
- *France, Germany and the New Europe, 1945-1963* (London: Oxford University Press) (1965)

Willett, R., *The Americanization of Germany 1945-1949* (London: Routledge) (1988)

Wilson, T., *The First Summit: Roosevelt and Churchill at Placentia Bay, 1941* (Kansas City: University Press of Kansas) (1991)

Woetzel, R., *The Nuremberg Trials in International Law (with a postlude on the Eichmann case)* (London: Stevens & Sons Ltd.) (1962)

Wolhforth, W.:

- *The Elusive Balance: Power and Perceptions During the Cold War* (Ithaca: Cornell University Press) (1993)
- 'New Evidence on Moscow's Cold War', *Diplomatic History* 21, no. 2 (Spring 1997)

Woodward, E. L., *British Foreign Policy in the Second World War,* Vol.5 (London: H.M.S.O.) (1976)

Woods R. and Jones, H., *The Dawning of the Cold War* (Athens, GA.: University of Georgia Press) (1991)

Woolner, D., *The Second Quebec Conference Revisited: Waging War, Formulating Peace: Canada, Great Britain, and the United States in 1944-1945* (New York: St. Martin's Press) (1998)

Yergin, D., *Shattered Peace*, rev. ed. (Harmondsworth: Penguin) (1990)

Young, E., *That Second Front: A Survey of Strategic and Political Factors* (London: W. H. Allen) (1942)

Young, J W., *France, the Cold War, and the Western Alliance, 1944-49* (Leicester: Leicester University Press) (1990)

Zubok, V. and Pleshakov C., *Inside the Kremlin's Cold War* (Cambridge, MA: Harvard University Press) (1996)

Index

Lightning Source UK Ltd.
Milton Keynes UK
21 January 2011

166116UK00002B/87/P

9 788895 145273